"Dodson's Spirit-led, gospel-centered, organically r
rare jewel. Jonathan is a good friend and an even be
to teach me much, and I pray the Spirit will use this
discipleship."

Matt Chandler, Lead Pastor, The Village Church, Dallas; author, *The Explicit Gospel*

"Nothing is more central to the global mission of the church than making disciples. This is at the very center of the gospel. *Gospel-Centered Discipleship* captures both the heart of the gospel and the essence of discipleship in the proper order. For too long we've put making disciples ahead of a clear understanding of the gospel. In cultures around the world, disciples lean away from the gospel toward religious performance or spiritual license. As a result, disciples burn out or drift from devotion to Jesus. *Gospel-Centered Discipleship* is an authentic re-centering of discipleship around the gospel of grace, in the context of community, for the mission of God. Don't miss it!"

S. Douglas Birdsall, Executive Chair, The Lausanne Movement

"Refreshingly honest and realistic, Dodson shares from experience the struggles and the bless-ings of making disciples. He does not give us a rule book, but gives practical teaching that can help every follower of Christ more effectively live out the gospel and the Great Commission."

Robert Coleman, Distinguished Professor of Evangelism and Discipleship,
Gordon-Conwell Theological Seminary; author, *Master Plan of Evangelism*

"Every church planter zealously runs into mission with a mandate from Jesus to make disciples of all nations. But what is a disciple? How are they formed? What needs to be done in order for a new church to make disciples? Dodson does a brilliant job of painting a picture of the head, heart, and hands of a disciple, as well as addressing how they are formed. This book provides a clear target for the church planter's mission to make disciples."

Scott Thomas, Founder, Gospel Coach; coauthor, *Gospel Coach: Shepherding Leaders to Glorify God*

"Jonathan strips away a stagnant view of discipleship and replaces it with something so refresh-ingly honest and deep, you find yourself craving it. This book will redefine all of your relation-ships with depth and transparency and Christ-centeredness. This isn't just God's design for discipleship—it's how we were designed to live. Jonathan just took discipleship from the spiritu-ally elite to dorm rooms and neighborhoods and coffee shops."

Jennie Allen, author, *Stuck: The Places We Get Stuck and the God Who Sets Us Free*

"Jonathan Dodson is the real deal! After reading the prequel to this book, we asked Jonathan to speak at our annual meeting. He blew us away with his grasp of the gospel and discipleship! If you want to take a deep dive into the mystery and joy of the gospel, this is the book for you. Jonathan will help you fight to keep the gospel the gospel. He will show you how to avoid the traps of performance and license. He will show you how to avoid believing a lie. And, most of all, he will help you to taste the sweetness of Jesus."

Patrick Morley, author, *The Man in the Mirror*; CEO, Man in the Mirror

"Takes us to the heart of the gospel and true discipleship, reminding us that the fight of faith is done in community in radical dependence on the power of the Spirit. It is a rare book that brings together clear theological thinking, stories of personal experience, and practical applica-tion. This book will be helpful to pastors, counselors, leaders, and anyone wanting a practical vision of gospel-centered life. It will surely challenge, convict, and encourage all who pick it up."

Jason Kovacs, Pastor of Counseling, The Austin Stone Community Church

"Jonathan has done us a huge favor in writing this book. As I read it, a growing passion to fight sin grew within me. I want to be a card-carrying member of a 'Fight Club' so that in community we can take sin seriously, encourage one another to believe the gospel deeply, and pray for each other to respond to the Holy Spirit passionately. What else can I say? This is an excellent book. Buy it. Read it. Do it."

Steve Timmis, coauthor, *Total Church* and *Everyday Church*; co-director, The Porterbrook Network, United Kingdom

"With all of the talk of gospel-centeredness these days, I'm thankful to see Jonathan unpack this topic with a clear, compelling, Spirit-empowered approach. He goes beyond just answering the question: 'What is gospel-centered?' to help us see how the gospel of grace really works in the details of everyday life. His clarification of the unhealthy divide between evangelism and discipleship will bring about a more holistic approach to gospel-centered discipleship. I know Jonathan and respect the fact that these are not just concepts or theories, but truths coming out of the practice of his own disciple-making ministry. I trust that this book will serve to further advance the work of discipleship that has the gospel of grace as its foundation."

Jeff Vanderstelt, author, *Saturate*; Lead Teaching Pastor, Bellevue Church, Bellevue, WA

"Jonathan cuts to the heart of the discipleship crisis we are facing by showing us that discipleship isn't an optional response to Jesus. Rather, it's embracing 'a whole way of following Jesus Christ as Lord in the whole of life.' This book will stir your heart and awaken in you the places the Good News is calling to reflect the likeness of Jesus. On top of this, his 'grace agenda' will push you to live out the multiplying principle we see at work in the Great Commission."

Mike Breen, author, *Creating a Discipleship Culture*; leader, 3DM Ministries

"One of the most healthy trends in the church today is a renewed focus on 'making disciples.' Jonathan Dodson has added an invaluable contribution to that trend. He makes it clear that making disciples must be gospel-centered and must take place in community. But he not only reminds us that this is what *should* be happening, he tells us how to actually make it happen. This book will give you a practical and proven approach that can work in your ministry setting. Read it carefully, both for its biblical challenge and its hands on approach to ministry."

Stephen Smallman, author, *The Walk: Steps for New and Renewed Followers of Jesus*

"For the longest time, I have been hoping to see two books on discipleship. The first would be a practical resource for churches that, on the one hand, was serious about the kind of discipleship and accountability that are necessary for Christian growth and yet, on the other hand, would put forth the gospel of grace, not legalistic self-improvement, as the key to change. The second book I've wished for is one that would situate the task of discipleship specifically within the missional calling of the church. I was thrilled to discover that Jonathan Dodson has managed to write *both* of these books in one. In *Gospel-Centered Discipleship*, Jonathan pulls together all these different themes—gospel, mission, discipleship, church, and Spirit—into an integrated whole. And quite honestly, I don't know a better person for that task."

Abraham Cho, Assistant Pastor, Redeemer Presbyterian Church, New York

"I am grateful for Jonathan Dodson's new book *Gospel-Centered Discipleship*. He masterfully took the truth and beauty of the gospel and pushed it into an area of Christendom that is typically performance driven. I came away from this book understanding how to think about discipleship in a new way. I also love that the book isn't just theory; Dodson has clearly lived what he is teaching. The truth in this book has built my love for the Holy Spirit. It has challenged my thinking on community and discipleship. And it has effectively pushed my comprehension of the gospel to a new level."

Jessica Thompson, coauthor, *Give Them Grace: Dazzling Your Kids With the Love of Jesus*

"Dodson writes with conviction and leaves the reader with important truths and responses to ponder. There is nothing cheap about the gospel he promotes. In fact, it's all about the Jesus whom we profess and the Father we adore, who lead us to a life of victory in God's Spirit. Read *Gospel-Centered Discipleship* with an open heart and a willing spirit to sustain you!"

Stephen A. Macchia, Director, Pierce Center for Disciple-Building, Gordon-Conwell Theological Seminary; author, *Becoming A Healthy Disciple*

"What is often vague or implied in the phrase 'gospel-centered,' is rendered clear and convincing by Jonathan Dodson. Here is the practical how-to of heart change, teaching how souls are changed and not simply their wanton behaviors. The tools are all here: what we need to know, think, do, and most essentially *believe* about the gospel to live as a new creatures in Christ. This fills in the practical gaps of gospel-centered discipleship and gospel-centered living."

Rick James, Publisher, CruPress; author, *Jesus Without Religion*

"One of the greatest challenges facing the missional movement is for disciples to ground their identity in the gospel, not in their mission. *Gospel-Centered Discipleship* clearly shows how true discipleship starts with a new identity *in* Christ, not a new behavior *for* Christ. It is saturated with deep truth and is as practical as it is informational. This book is a game-changer."

Brandon Hatmaker, author; *Barefoot Church*; pastor, Austin New Church, Austin, Texas

"Jonathan knows that discipleship is of strategic importance in terms of the vitality, sustainability, and impact of the church. He also knows that to be true disciples we must become more like Jesus or else degenerate into religious ideology. *Gospel-Centered Discipleship* is a really helpful and fertile book for a critical time."

Alan Hirsch, Founder, Forge Mission Training Network

"If in your struggle against sin you've been beaten up by the duty-bound, legalistic, moralistic methods of contemporary discipleship or enslaved by the licentious approach to holiness by proponents of cheap grace, then *Gospel-Centered Discipleship* is for you! Dodson calls us to join the fight against sin, legalism, and license by believing everything the gospel says about who God is for us in Christ, and how he is conforming us to the image of His Son. Read this book. Form a 'club.' And begin fighting sin for the glory of God and your joy in Christ."

Juan Sanchez, Preaching Pastor, High Pointe Baptist Church, Austin, Texas

"I am a big fan of Jonathan Dodson and grateful for this book. The church is desperate for this vision of grace-based, gospel-centered discipleship. I know I am! The guilt-ridden, shame-based, discipleship trail I stumbled on for years left me tired, defeated, and self-righteous. The discovery of gospel-centrality in my journey as a disciple and in making disciples, like this book reinforces and lays out so beautifully, saved my life, gave me hope, and, quite simply, changed everything. Gospel-centered sanctification and gospel-centered ecclesiology are like two lost continents to the current church. Thanks, Jonathan, for your work to help blaze the trail!"

John W. Bryson, Teaching Pastor, Fellowship Memphis, Memphis, Tennessee

"A timely book about gospel-centered accountability in an age of anonymity and shallow relationships. Dodson has done a masterful job highlighting how the Holy Spirit uses gospel truth to give us new, Christ-centered affections that dispel our thirst for sin. Moreover, he helps us see how we can come alongside each other to unearth the deeper heart-idols that drive our more obvious sins. For those still playing at religion through superficial, pseudo-accountability, this book is a welcome killjoy. You'll never look at accountability the same way again."

Luke Gilkerson, Internet Director, Covenant Eyes; blogger, Breaking Free

"*Gospel-Centered Discipleship* is a breath of fresh air. Dodson does an excellent job of combining theology and praxis. Highly recommended for those seeking to build a discipleship culture in their church."

Jon Tyson, Acting Parish Pastor, Trinity Grace Church, New York, New York

FOREWORD BY MATT CHANDLER

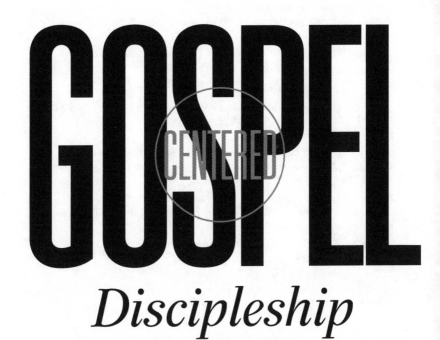

GOSPEL

Discipleship

Jonathan K. Dodson

∷ CROSSWAY

WHEATON, ILLINOIS

Trade paperback ISBN: 978-1-4335-3021-0
PDF ISBN: 978-1-4335-3022-7
Mobipocket ISBN: 978-1-4335-3023-4
ePub ISBN: 978-1-4335-3024-1

Library of Congress Cataloging-in-Publication Data

Dodson, Jonathan K.
Gospel-centered discipleship / Jonathan K. Dodson ; foreword by Matt Chandler.
   p. cm.
  Includes bibliographical references and index.
  ISBN 978-1-4335-3021-0 (tp)
  1. Discipling (Christianity). I. Title.
BV4520.D63   2012
248.4—dc23   2011037084

Crossway is a publishing ministry of Good News Publishers.

VP		24	23	22	21	20	19	18	17	16	15
19	18	17	16	15	14	13	12	11	10	9	8	7

This book is dedicated to my remarkable wife,
Robie.
*With you I have discovered gospel depths that have
strengthened and sweetened our union
to enjoy eleven years of friendship, marriage, and ministry.
Sweetheart, you remind me of Jesus every single day,
without saying a word.*

CONTENTS

FOREWORD

As a pastor, I constantly pray and engage the people of the Village Church to keep what is "of first importance" at the center of their thinking, in both their justification and their sanctification. Over the years, I have become painfully aware that people tend to drift away from the gospel soon after their conversion and begin to try their hand at sanctification. In other words, they operate as if the gospel saves them but doesn't play a role in sanctifying them. In the end, people become exhausted and miss out on the joy of knowing and walking with the Spirit of God. They miss out on intimacy with Jesus.

This is why I think Paul keeps preaching the gospel to people who already know it. He does it in Romans, 1 Corinthians, Galatians, Ephesians, Philippians, and Colossians. Over and over, he preaches the gospel to people who know the gospel. Why does he do that? He tells us in 1 Corinthians 15:1–2: "Now I would remind you, brothers, of the gospel I preached to you, which you received"—*past tense*—"in which you stand"—*perfect tense*—which tells us that the Corinthian disciples stood in the gospel in the past and continued to stand in the gospel. We see that the gospel was received, and now it is holding them up. So the gospel not only saves me, but it also sustains me. Paul continues: "and by which you are being saved"—*present tense*. The gospel is good news for our past, it continues to be good news for the present, and will remain that way for all eternity.

The book you are holding is of significant help in keeping the gospel of first importance. Jonathan is going to clearly and biblically unpack how the gospel plays the lead in not only how we are saved, but also how we are sanctified. I have used this material in small group discipleship for over a year and am grateful that it is now being published. I have witnessed a great deal of fruit in my own life as well as in the lives of those I walk closely with. The chapter on the Holy Spirit was especially powerful for me, and I have found myself going back and reading it over and over again.

As a pastor and a man who desires to lead other men into maturity, I wish there were more resources like *Gospel-Centered Discipleship*. Dodson's Spirit-led, gospel-centered, organically relational, and authentic book is such a rare jewel. I am grateful for Jonathan. He is a good friend and an even better ally in the gospel. God has used him to teach me much, and I pray the Spirit would use this book in your hands to challenge and change your heart and the way you view and *do* discipleship.

Matt Chandler
Lead Pastor, The Village Church,
Flower Mound, TX

ACKNOWLEDGMENTS

I am incredibly grateful that I get to witness the power of the Spirit through the gospel in my local church, Austin City Life. Thank you all for being the church with me and for encouraging me to put these ideas on paper. Your fight for faith in the gospel causes many to look on and give glory to our great God. It is an honor to serve Jesus with you.

I extend a special thanks to Sam Kleb for his editorial assistance in an early version of the book and to J. T. Caldwell who read several versions of the current manuscript and offered encouragement along the way.

Also, thanks to my Re:Lit editor, Matt Johnson, who pushed me to make this a better book, and Mattie Wolf (what a great name for an editor), who tightened my manuscript up.

I am deeply grateful for "the good deposit" of the gospel I received from my wonderful parents. No son could ask for more in a mother and father. Thanks, Mom and Dad!

Robie, thank you for teaching me so much about God's grace, for your unparalleled love and companionship, and for our lifelong partnership in fighting to believe and spread the good news of God's remarkable grace. Finally, thank you, Father, for your enduring love; Jesus Christ, for being both my Lord and my Christ; and Spirit, for making me new and giving me eyes to peer into the beauties of the gospel.

INTRODUCTION

This book is the result of my struggle as a disciple of Jesus. Over the past three decades, I have failed in countless ways to obey and honor Jesus. I have wandered the wasteland of religion in an attempt to earn the unearnable favor of God. I have chased the pleasures of the world in an attempt to satisfy my infinite longings with finite things. Neither the legalistic rules of religion nor license from rules in worldly living have satisfied. These twists and turns on the path of discipleship have not honored Christ. Yet, despite my failures, year after year the desire to honor and obey Christ has not withered. In fact, it has grown amid failure.

Along the way, I've come to understand that following Jesus *alone* is not really what it means to be a disciple. Both the church and the parachurch taught me that being a disciple means *making* disciples. I was told that this meant two primary things. First, I should be active in "sharing my faith." Second, I should find Christians who are younger in the faith to demonstrate how to be older in the faith. It took me quite a while to realize that this practice of making disciples was incomplete. Discipleship is not a code word for evangelism, nor is it a hierarchical system for spiritual growth, a way for professional Christians to pass on their best practices to novice Christians. *Making disciples requires not only "sharing our faith," but also sharing our lives—failures and successes, disobedience and obedience.*

Professional vs. Novice Discipleship

Real discipleship is messy, imperfect, and honest. I wanted clean, "perfect," and limited honesty. I preferred to disclose only my successes, to pass on my accumulated wisdom and knowledge while hiding my foolishness and ignorance. It's not that I wasn't making disciples; people gobbled up my platitudes and piety. The problem was the *kind* of disciples I was making, disciples who could share their faith but not their failures.

Why did I embrace this kind of discipleship? Who was to blame—the church or the parachurch? Neither. It was my fault. Although I didn't understand it at the time, my motivation for obeying Jesus had shifted from grace to works. It progressed from attempting to earn God's favor, to gaining the favor of my disciples. "Discipleship" had become a way to leverage my identity and worth in relationship with others. I was comfortable on the pedestal dispensing wisdom and truth. The more disciples I made, the better I felt about myself. My motivation for discipleship was a mixture of genuine love for God and lust for praise. I sincerely loved God and wanted others to fall more deeply in love with him, but my motives weren't always pure. I quickly became a disciple who lacked authenticity and community.

Don't get me wrong, there were good intentions and good fruit from these relationships, but in a sense, I was still following Jesus *alone*. The professional/novice relationship created a comfortable distance from admitting my failures in genuine community. I stood at the top of the stairs of discipleship, peering down at those who sat at my feet instead of sitting in the living room with my fellow disciples, where I belonged. I put the best foot forward and hid the ugly one. As a result, disciple became more of a verb than a noun, less of an identity and more of an activity. The center of discipleship subtly shifted from relationships centered on Christ to an activity centered on what I knew.

The Gospel Is for Disciples, Not Just "Sinners"

Fortunately, the gospel is big enough to handle my failures, and Jesus is forgiving enough for my distortions of what it means to follow him. In fact, the gospel of grace is so big and strong that it has reshaped my understanding of discipleship. As I continued to "disciple" and read the Bible, I was struck by the fact that the disciples of Jesus were always attached to other disciples. They lived in authentic community. They confessed their sins and struggles alongside their successes—questioning their Savior and casting out demons. They continually came back to Jesus as their Master and eventually as their Redeemer. As the disciples grew in maturity, they did not grow beyond the need for their Redeemer. They returned to him for forgiveness. As they began to multiply, the communities that they formed did not graduate from the gospel that forgave and saved them. Instead, churches formed around their common need for Jesus. The gospel of Jesus became the unifying center of the church. As a result, the communities that formed preached Jesus, not only to those outside the church but also to one another within the church.[1] I began to realize that Jesus is not merely the start and standard for salvation, but that he is the beginning, middle, and end of my salvation. He is my salvation, not just when I was six, but every second of every day. In the gospel, Jesus gives me himself, his redemptive benefits, and the church to share those benefits with. As it turns out, the gospel is for disciples, not just for "sinners;" it saves and transforms people in relationship, not merely individuals who go it alone.

It slowly became apparent to me that the gospel of Christ was where I was meant to find my identity, not in impressing God or others with my discipling skill. Refusing to share my life with others, especially my failures, was a refusal to allow the gospel of Christ to accomplish its full breadth of redemption in me. Very simply, God was leading me into a kind of discipleship with the gospel at the center—a constant, gracious repetition of repentance and faith in Jesus, who is sufficient for my failures and strong for my successes. The wonderful news of the gospel is that Jesus frees us from trying to impress God or others because he has impressed God on our behalf. We can tell people our sins because our identity doesn't hang on what they think of us. We can be imperfect Christians because we cling to a perfect Christ. In this kind of discipleship, Jesus is at the center with the church huddled around him. We give and receive the gospel of Jesus to one another for our forgiveness and formation. In sum, discipleship is both gospel centered and community shaped.

Gospel-centered discipleship is not about how we perform but who we are—*imperfect people, clinging to a perfect Christ, being perfected by the Spirit.* As a result, I no longer stand at the top of the stairs but sit in the living room, where I can share my faith and my unfaith, my obedience and disobedience, my success and failure. As we give and receive the gospel, we don't linger in imperfection, unbelief, disobedience, and failure. The Bible repeatedly tells us to fight. We have to fight to believe this gospel. Otherwise, we will slide back into individualistic, indifferent, or professionalized discipleship. This fight is a fight of faith. It is a struggle to believe what the gospel truly promises over what sin deceitfully promises. We need to remind one another that Jesus has not called us to performance or indifference but to faith in him. We need relationships that are so shaped by the gospel that we will exhort and encourage one another to trust Jesus every single day. We need gospel-centered discipleship.

Gospel-Centered Discipleship
(and How the Book Unfolds)

Knowingly or unknowingly, everyone puts something in the center of discipleship. In fact, everyone has a habit of putting rules in the middle of their relationships. Some like to keep the rules while others prefer to break them. I want us to replace the center (not necessarily the rules) with grace. This grace originates with the Father, flows through the Son, and settles on us in the Spirit. We can't get to it without going right through Jesus, which is why discipleship is Jesus- or gospel-centered. Discipleship is about trusting Jesus, believing his gospel. While this may sound simple enough, the problem is that we all struggle to understand what trusting Jesus or believing the gospel really looks like. In addition, the notion that we should fight for this belief is rare. I have tried to show how we can believe the gospel and why it is every bit worth fighting for. Why and how we believe the gospel is the burden of this book.

Here is how the book unfolds. Part 1 forms the base of discipleship by providing a definition for disciple. Chapter 1 situates gospel-centered discipleship within the broader framework of disciple making, paying particular attention to the distinction between evangelism and discipleship. Is this a helpful or harmful distinction? How does gospel-centered discipleship address it? Chapter 2 builds on the definition of discipleship by identifying its clear goal—the image of Jesus. We all care about image, about the way people see us. Often this image falls short of Jesus, yet we are willing to strive for it. What must be done so the noble, beautiful image of Christ is revealed in us?

Part 2 addresses the heart of a disciple. Chapter 3 explores where we go off center our fighting by focusing on misguided motivations in discipleship. In turn, chapter 4 calls us away from these extremes into gospel-centered motivations for following Jesus. With the gospel at the center of discipleship, we can live as Jesus intended—with faith in Jesus to produce the image of Jesus. Chapter 5 explains where these motivations come from—the power and presence of the Holy Spirit. Unfortunately, the Spirit has been widely neglected by many Christians. Without the Spirit we cannot believe the gospel.

Part 3 tackles the practical aspect of discipleship by showing how we can apply the gospel in community and on mission. With proper motivations in place, chapter 6 turns to the communal nature of discipleship. If we aren't careful, we'll follow Jesus on our own. Failure to grasp the community focus of the gospel can cut us off from the grace God gives through the church. This reminds us that discipleship is a community project because the gospel redeems a people. Jesus created and redeemed us as people in relationship, not individuals in isolation. Instead of following alone, we can fight the good fight of faith with the church. Chapter 7 offers a practical way to apply the gospel in everyday life. It is a call for fight clubs—small, simple, reproducible groups of people who meet together regularly to help one another beat up sin and believe the gospel. Fight clubs have been crucial in my life and in my church. I hope and pray that you'll find them helpful, too, that you'll form a fight club and start fighting with the church for faith in the gospel. Finally, chapter 8 explains how to nurture and multiply truly gospel-centered disciples in your church or ministry.

On one hand, this book was very easy to write. As if guided by a "muse" to bring my thoughts, beliefs, feelings, and experiences together in written form, I often watched words flow freely onto the screen. Periodically, I was provoked to heart-enthralled worship as I struck geysers of insight, repentance, and joy.

On the other hand, this book was, at times, difficult to write. For one, I had to taste the bitterness of my own sin as I reflected on my failures. In addition, I faced the challenge of writing something that is neither purely practical nor theological but both. I would like to write a biblical theology of discipleship; however, several helpful ones have already been written.[2] *Following the Master: A Biblical Theology of Discipleship* by Michael J. Wilkins and *The Gospel Commission: Recovering God's Strategy for Making Disciples* by Michael Horton both address this topic. Therefore, in this book I have labored to integrate theology with everyday practice put into accessible form. For that reason, I have included theological sources in the notes, in the hope that many will read the sources. Finally, I pray that you will read this book in conversation with your heavenly Father, pausing to reflect, repent, and rejoice wherever the Holy Spirit prompts you. As you read, may God not only prompt but also cause you to "grow in the grace and knowledge of our Lord and Savior Jesus Christ" (2 Pet. 3:18)!

PART ONE

Defining Discipleship

1

MAKING DISCIPLES: EVANGELISM OR DISCIPLESHIP?

I'll never forget my introduction to discipleship. I had been a Christian for fourteen years, and was returning from a semester of Bible school at Capernwray Hall in Carnforth, England. My return was not voluntary. I was kicked out. The reason I left was the reason I went—an inordinate desire for female affection.

Months prior to my departure from Capernwray, I had been through the most devastating experience of my life to date. A lust-ridden relationship with a girl I met at college came crashing down all around me. I was nineteen. Big deal, right? It gets bigger. I was a whirlwind of emotions, unable to separate love from lust. One night my girlfriend broke the news that her father had abused her growing up, and that she was going to have to return home due to her poor grades.

What should I do? I couldn't let her return to an abusive home. I took some time to pray and consider the best way to respond. In my mind, there was really only one appropriate conclusion—to marry my girlfriend, rescuing her from abuse. We eloped. Confident of my noble action, I couldn't wait to break the news to my parents. I just knew they would be proud of me. I will never forget my mother's shrill cry on the other end of the payphone when I called to tell her the good news. In between sobs, she told me that my girlfriend wasn't telling me everything. Within days the truth came out. My girlfriend had intentionally deceived me about the abuse in order to "keep me." Aware her failing grades would require a move home, separating her from me and therefore threatening the loss of our relationship, she decided to lie to me. She fabricated the story about her father's abusive behavior to get me to intervene. There was no abuse, but there was a marriage. What was I to do? Who was this person? How could true love deceive me and go along with our marriage under false pretense?

Confused, angry, and heartbroken, I returned home where I sought my parents' counsel and healing love. Within two weeks, we had agreed to terminate the "marriage." The court passed a rare annulment, but nothing could annul the pain. I felt as though someone had taken a shotgun to my heart, shattering my emotions into a thousand pieces. The road to recovery would take many twists.

As a Christian, I knew that God hated my sin, but I had no idea how much he loved me. I shipped off to Bible school in England to try to figure things out, where I struggled with questions like: *Who is God in the mess of my life? What can I do with this gnawing pain of betrayal? What does God think of my shameful Christian failure?* I prayed and cried a lot but eventually sought comfort in a lesser savior. Although my escape to England numbed the pain, I quickly ran into the arms of another lover. I started dating a girl, sneaking out with her at night to go to the local pub. Eventually, I was caught making out with her on the premises and was kicked out of Bible school the day before the semester was over. Did I mention that this was the place where my parents had met, twenty years earlier? I made another phone call to them, this time fully aware of my failure. I limped home in shame. To my parents' credit, they had taught and loved me well. This failure was all my own doing. I reentered college with a gaping emotional wound and a sincere desire to improve, to restore the reputation of Christ in my life, to get it right.

When I returned home from England, I found a best friend and got a discipler. My friend would hold me accountable and my discipler would help me mature. The three of us met regularly for Bible study. As a disciple, I was taught how to study the Bible, share my faith, and cultivate character. As I understood it, discipleship was about maturing as a Christian, which is why the notion that I, too, could or should make disciples was pretty foreign. But somewhere along the way, I was told that *evangelism* is also discipleship, and that all Christians are supposed to evangelize in order to "make disciples." Brushing aside the confusion between evangelism and discipleship, I went for it. I began to evangelize non-Christians *and* disciple Christians. My spirits lifted. I was on a better track, making things right. Along the way, I pondered how I could have sinned so much *as a Christian*. I tacitly concluded it was a lack of discipleship. Some might say the reason I struggled with sin so much as a Christian was because I only became a *convert* when I was six but finally became a *disciple* when I was twenty.

I've shared part of my story to illustrate the confusion over the meaning of discipleship and clarify its meaning along the way. Discipleship has become a catchall term that means different things for different people. When some people use the word, they think of a process for maturing Christians, perhaps what I experienced after returning from England (which I will come back to later). This kind of maturity might happen through a discipleship program or by meeting someone for coffee to discuss spiritual matters or to study the Bible. Others consider discipleship an evangelistic method. In this view, discipleship isn't about maturing Christians; it's about making Christians. Discipleship is sharing the gospel to win people to Christ. Evangelists make disciples. Entire organizations and churches are subtly divided by these two approaches to discipleship. Some organizations focus on maturing Christians, while others focus on making Christians. The former is about discipleship and the latter about evangelism. The evangelist proclaims the gospel to make converts, and the discipler teaches converts how to grow into disciples, hence the clarifying phrase, "evangelism and discipleship."

The problem, however, is that this phrase is not clarifying at all. The attempt to clarify discipleship by separating it from evangelism actually muddies the waters. The problem is twofold. First, both evangelists and the disciplers refer to their ministries as "disciple making." Should discipleship be understood as evangelizing non-Christians or the maturing of Christians? Second, and more importantly, the separation of evangelism from discipleship implies that "sharing the gospel" with non-Christians is an activity that is unnecessary with Christians. It intimates that the gospel doesn't need to be shared with disciples. This dichotomy surfaces a false view of the gospel, namely that the gospel has the power to save but not to sanctify. It assumes that the gospel functions like a space shuttle's external fuel tank, falling away after the shuttle has launched us into God's orbit. The gospel, however, is more like an internal engine, always propelling us into God's presence. The gospel is necessary for getting right and doing right with God, for salvation and sanctification.

What, then, is the truth about discipleship? In this chapter, I will try to clarify these two issues surrounding discipleship by establishing a definition for the word *disciple*. With a clear definition in place, we will proceed to show how the gospel integrates, not dichotomizes, evangelism and discipleship. As I will show throughout this book, understanding the role of the gospel in discipleship can make a huge difference in our lives. It certainly has in mine! Once a gospel-centered definition of discipleship is established, we will turn our attention to how the gospel actually makes disciples.

Defining Discipleship

The word *disciple* is used more frequently than *Christian* to refer to believers in the Bible.[1] This repeated usage tells us that disciple is a fundamental category for Christians. We are disciples first and parents, employees, pastors, deacons, and spouses second. Disciple is an identity; everything else is a role. Our roles are temporary but our identity will last forever. Marvelous. If this is true, it is incredibly important to have a sound definition for the word *disciple*.

There are three aspects that comprise a disciple's identity. The first is *rational*. Popular descriptions of the word *disciple* are often taken from the definition of the Greek word, *mathetes*, which is rendered "student or pupil." Interestingly, the Greek philosopher Socrates eschewed *mathetes* as a term for designating his relationship with his followers. This was primarily due to its rational connotation among the Sophists. The Sophists reduced the meaning of *disciple* to an exchange of information between master and student.[2] While *mathetes* certainly includes the rational meaning implied in the student-teacher relationship, the biblical definition of disciple cannot be determined by classical Greek usage alone. Rather, the whole of biblical theology, and Jesus's way of making disciples in particular, should shape our definition. Michael Wilkins offers this perspective in his foundational biblical theology of discipleship, *Following the Master:*

A Biblical Theology of Discipleship. He notes that the meaning of "disciple" should not be restricted to a dictionary definition alone: "The type of relationship is not to be found within the inherent meaning in *mathetes* but within *the dynamic created by the master and the kind of commitment to him*" (emphasis added).[3] What kind of dynamic existed between Jesus and his disciples? It certainly included a rational dynamic. Jesus appealed to the reason of his followers by instructing them through sermons, stories, and object lessons. He labored to teach them the gospel of the kingdom of God (Matt. 4:23; 9:35; 24:14; Mark 1:14–15).

However, like Socrates, Jesus did not view his disciples as mere students. He viewed them as family: "'Who is my mother, and who are my brothers?' And stretching out his hand *toward his disciples*, he said, 'Here are my mother and my brothers!'" (Matt. 12:48–49). For Jesus, discipleship was rational and *relational*, the second aspect of being a disciple. His relationship with the disciples was based on truth and grace (John 1:14–17). He taught them the gospel and embodied its grace for them in everyday life. God humbled himself in Jesus to share everyday life with everyday people. He chose twelve disciples from various vocations ranging from fisherman to tax man and shared everything with them! Jesus shared his meals, his heart, his teachings, his sufferings, and his hopes for the future with these men, all while taking road trips, mountain hikes, and moving toward his urban martyrdom. Imagine how strong and intimate these relationships were after three years! The disciples had become family. Yet, Jesus's truth and grace was not restricted to his immediate family of disciples. It was meant to overflow. The family was intended to grow. We might say Jesus's discipleship relationships had a grace agenda.

The ~~Great~~ (Gospel) Commission

Jesus's grace agenda reveals a third aspect in the identity of a disciple—*missional*.* A disciple is rational (learner), relational (family), and missional (missionary).[4] All three aspects of discipleship are expressed in Jesus's so-called Great Commission in Matthew 28:18–20: "And Jesus came and said to them, 'All authority in heaven and on earth has been given to me. Go therefore and make disciples of all nations, baptizing them in the name of the Father and of the Son and of the Holy Spirit, teaching them to observe all that I have commanded you. And behold, I am with you always, to the end of the age.'"[5]

Gospel Going

In this commission, Jesus reveals his agenda to make disciples, not just of the twelve but also of every ethnic group in the world. How would his audacious agenda be accomplished? Jesus tells us that by going, baptizing, and teaching we can fulfill his commission. These three participles modify the main verb "make disciples." Going reflects the sent nature of a disciple. Disciples are sent to make more disciples: "Go therefore and make disciples. . . . " (Matt. 28:19).[6] The main point isn't to go (in your effort), but that we are sent (under Jesus's authority and in Jesus's power). Jesus is the ground of our going. When Jesus sends, he sends not merely to evangelize but in his power to make disciples. Under his authority, the so-called Great Comission begins with Jesus, not our great effort, and ends with Jesus—"I am with you always, to the end of the age" (Matt. 28:20). The mission of making disciples starts and finishes with Jesus. As we will see, this is what truly makes the Great Comis-

---

*I plan on writing a follow-up book that focuses exclusively on the missional aspect of discipleship.

sion great—Jesus! Hence, it would be more accurate to refer to it as the Gospel Comission.

Assuming a disciple is on mission, how are we supposed to make disciples? Should we start a discipleship program? What did Jesus expect his disciples to do? In his classic book, *The Master Plan of Evangelism*, Robert Coleman answers precisely this question: "His [Jesus's] concern was not with programs to reach the multitudes, but with men whom the multitudes would follow. . . . Men were to be his method of winning the world to God."[7] Men were his method. Men and women sharing the gospel with other men and women is how Jesus would spread his grace agenda. They did this, like their Master, by communicating a rationally coherent gospel. Jesus sent the twelve and the seventy on missions to proclaim the gospel of the kingdom. We might say that they "evangelized" by announcing the arrival of God's rule and reign in Christ. They joined Jesus in calling people to repentance, and the number of disciples increased (Luke 6:17). The disciples made disciples by going with the gospel.

Gospel Baptizing

As the disciples went, they also baptized. Baptism reflects all three aspects of a disciple's identity, with particular emphasis on missional. First, baptism is a sign that we have learned the gospel. It signifies our identification with Christ in his death as we are lowered into his "watery grave," and identification with his life, where we are raised up into his resurrection life (Rom. 6:4). In baptism, we are meant to see that Jesus's death and resurrection becomes our death and resurrection. The life that emerges from the baptismal waters is a life that is dead to sin and alive to God. In this sense, baptism is not merely a ceremony but a symbol of the gospel. Second, we are baptized into two overlapping communities. The first is the divine community of the Trinity: "Baptizing them in the name of the Father and of the Son and of the Holy Spirit" (Matt: 28:19). The second community is the church: "For in one Spirit we were all baptized into one body" (1 Cor. 12:13). Baptism results in our participation in a new, spiritual family—the family of the Trinity. Jesus is the entry point into the divine community and the head of our new community. When we learn Jesus, we are baptized into his family, both human and divine. Third, baptism is missional because it is the outcome of obedience to the Gospel Commission. If sent disciples don't share the gospel in the power and authority of Jesus, then people don't get to respond by repentance, faith, and baptism. If sent disciples do live out their identity, sharing Jesus, then people are baptized in vivid commemoration of their faith in Jesus Christ as Lord. In a sense, baptism is the end of the Gospel Commission and, at the same time, it is its beginning. Baptism *begins* our participation in the wonderful gospel mission. Whenever someone is baptized, another disciple is sent in the power and authority of Jesus to join the mission of making disciples of all nations.

Once we become his disciples, our challenges don't disappear. Although Jesus's death and resurrection becomes our death and resurrection by faith, we often exchange our new life for the old life. We temporarily place our faith in something or someone other than Jesus. One of the great challenges of disciples is to walk out our new life of Christ, enjoying his victory over sin. God gives us the gift of repentance so that we can continually return to our new life in Christ and enjoy communion with him. The disciple who fights to believe the gospel and live out his or her baptism becomes a witness to the power of the gospel. The fight to be who we are in Christ is what this book is all about. I want to encourage you to be disciples who believe what God has said about you and what he has done for you in the gospel. To summarize, the first two directives of the Gospel Commission, going and baptizing, primarily reflect the relational and missional aspects of a disciple. They also reveal that when a rational gospel is truly believed, a relational and missional disciple is made. We make disciples by gospel going and gospel baptizing.

Gospel Teaching

Jesus's Commission is further described as "teaching them to observe all that I have commanded" (Matt. 28:20). What is the teaching Christ commanded?[8] John Nolland comments: "In Matthew 'all that I have commanded you' has in mind the teaching of Jesus *in the Gospel as directed to the disciples*."[9] The teaching is the gospel including the breadth of the redemptive, Christ-centered story and the depth of later doctrinal reflection on that story. It is the story of how the good news unfolds and what that story means. The meaning of the story is unlocked for the disciples when they discover that it is wrapped up in the person and work of Jesus himself: "And beginning with Moses and all the Prophets, he interpreted to them in all the Scriptures the things concerning *himself*" (Luke 24:27). Jesus is both the story-teller and the point of the story. He showed the disciples how the Old Testament revealed his suffering, death, and resurrection. Moreover, our aim is to not only teach the gospel but also to observe the gospel. We are to teach disciples to observe all that Christ commanded. As the point of the story, Jesus should be applied to our lives, which is precisely what he calls for: "Thus it is written, that the Christ should suffer and on the third day rise from the dead, *and that repentance and forgiveness of sins should be proclaimed in his name to all nations*, beginning from Jerusalem"

(Luke 24:46–47). Christ-centered repentance and forgiveness is something to be heard and applied, not just once, but for the entirety of a disciple's life. At the risk of oversimplification, we could say that the Gospel Commission commands us to learn the gospel *by the gospel*. We learn the breadth and depth of the good news by continually situating ourselves in it, through repentance and faith in Jesus Christ as Lord. Jesus is the gospel of our teaching and observing. It is this understanding of the gospel that makes disciples, which is why it would be better to refer to the commission as the "Gospel Commission." The Gospel Commission sends us to teach and observe the gospel.

With this all too brief explanation of the Gospel Commission directives, we must conclude that the gospel isn't just for evangelism, the initial making of disciples. It is also for discipleship, the continual making of disciples. Jesus's view of discipleship is radically gospel centered. The gospel is for not-yet disciples and already disciples. The gospel people believe to be baptized is the same gospel people believe to be sanctified (through the work of the Spirit). Followers of Jesus make *and* mature disciples by going with the gospel, baptizing disciples into gospel community, and teaching the gospel. We are to go in the power of the gospel, baptize into the grace of the gospel, and teach the Person of the gospel. Jesus is the ground of our going, the goal of our baptizing, and the gospel of our teaching. Making disciples is radically Jesus centered. This is how we make disciples—gospel going, gospel baptizing, gospel teaching.

If making disciples happens through gospel-centered going, baptizing, and teaching, the semantic distinction between evangelism and discipleship is superfluous. Disciples are made, whether for the first or the fiftieth time, through the gospel. Jesus's real concern was not evangelism versus discipleship, but the good news. Both are a product of the gospel. The evangelism/discipleship debate misses the point of the Gospel Commission. Jesus's Commission is not mission centered but gospel centered. It focuses on proclaiming the gospel to not-yet disciples and teaching the gospel to already disciples. Jesus puts the gospel first, which leads to making and maturing disciples. He does not call people to evangelize first, making discipleship an optional second. Both evangelism and discipleship are gospel motivated.

When the Gospel Commission is understood rightly, the dichotomy between evangelism and discipleship becomes significant. This dichotomy removes the gospel of grace from discipleship while maintaining its centrality in evangelism. But as we have seen, the gospel is central to making disciples! This clarification helps me reinterpret my initial encounter with discipleship. I now see that spiritual growth as a disciple isn't what rectified the moral failures of my past. No, the death and life of Jesus is what rectifies my past, forgiving all my sins, Christian and pre-Christian. Therefore, it is continual trust in his death and life for my sin and righteousness that matures me, drawing me deeper and deeper into an ever-present hope of acceptance before God. This hope is Jesus Christ as my Lord and Redeemer, not a better moral track record. When we absorb the radical gospel focus of the Gospel Commission, it compels the mission of making disciples who, in turn, preach and teach the gospel of grace to others.

Christians who internalize the gospel of grace more and more are compelled to spread the gospel more and more. The problem, however, is that very often the gospel we preach and teach is malnourished. In evangelism, the gospel is frequently reduced to a spiritual ticket to guarantee a reservation in heaven. This view of the gospel makes joining the mission of God or submitting to Jesus Christ as Lord optional. It teaches us that the gospel is all we need to cash in the ticket when death comes knocking at our door.

When this view of the gospel is adopted in discipleship, it relegates the gospel to evangelistic activity. As a result, discipleship must become something different. We force it to set itself apart by focusing on something more "advanced" like theology, piety, or social justice. These views on evangelism and discipleship stem from a gross misunderstanding of the Gospel Commission, namely that the Commission is centered on either the mission of soul winning or the mission of Christian maturing. These interpretations are gospel anemic. The Gospel Commission is not evangelism or discipleship centered; it is gospel centered. Rightly understood, the gospel calls the evangelized to more than belief to obtain a ticket, and disciples to more than spreading an anemic gospel which must be beefed up through spiritual disciplines or social justice. Jesus's disciples would never have made this gross error. They knew the gospel was of kingdom proportions, animating and laying claim to all of life. The gospel makes all-encompassing demands, and what the gospel demands, it supplies. The disciples knew that the gospel, not mission, was the invigorating power of Jesus's Commission. This is why they devoted their lives to the mission of making disciples by going, baptizing, and teaching *the gospel*.

Therefore, when we go, baptize, and teach others, we express all three aspects of discipleship—rational, relational, and missional. As learner, family, and missionary, every disciple joins Jesus's grace agenda by baptizing and teaching others the gospel, for the first or the fiftieth time. Recalling Wilkins's insistence that the definition of a disciple should be determined by "the dynamic created by the master," we conclude that Jesus's definition of a disciple includes the three aspects of rational, relational, and missional. These aspects are expressed through the communication of gospel truth (rational) within everyday relationships of love (relational) with a grace agenda to baptize people into the name of the Father, Son, and Holy Spirit (missional). *A disciple of Jesus, then, is someone who learns the gospel, relates in the gospel, and communicates the gospel.* In short, disciples are gospel centered.[10]

The Gospel Makes *and* Matures Disciples

A disciple of Jesus is someone who learns the gospel, relates in the gospel, and communicates the gospel. This definition of disciple shows us that the gospel both makes and matures disciples. We see this in Jesus's ministry. Jesus proclaimed the same gospel to the crowds that he taught to the disciples. He did not have the twelve on a special, gospel-plus track to study advanced subject matter. The gospel is for undergraduates and graduates because nobody ever graduates from the gospel. Jesus taught the same gospel of the kingdom to sinners and saints. Why? Because his agenda of grace is the only solution to our common predicament of sin, Christian or non-Christian. Both desperately need the forgiving, reconciling, and restoring power of the gospel to know and enjoy God, not just once but for a lifetime.

In light of this understanding of discipleship, I did not become a disciple at twenty; I became a disciple upon conversion to Jesus Christ, at age six. My collegiate sins did not betray a failure to become a disciple upon my conversion; they betrayed a failure to grasp the gospel in sanctification. We aren't converted at the outset of the Christian life only to join the gospel-plus track a little later as a disciple. What I was missing was not a new set of relationships to usher me into Christian maturity (with a discipler and an accountability partner) but a deep understanding of the gospel of grace. What I needed was a deeper comprehension of the cross and the resurrection. I needed to know that Jesus's sacrifice is sufficient, not just for pre-Christian failures but for post-Christian, lifelong failures. Jesus died to set me free from judgment by embracing my judgment on the cross. Riddled with guilt and sin, and a dichotomous view of discipleship, I could not grasp the freeing forgiveness purchased for me at the cross of Christ. Unaware of my union with Christ, his enduring approval seemed like something I had to regain. I did not grasp the present tense power of a Jesus "delivered up for our trespasses and raised for our justification" (Rom. 4:25), which confers forgiveness and acceptance not only in the past but also in the present.

The power of God's reckless love and remarkable grace could not pull me out of sin into repentance because, in some way, I perceived that love and grace as restricted for better men. I felt I had transgressed in my new life in Christ, forever trapped in a struggle to return to the new. I failed to believe Romans 6:6–7: "We know that our old self was crucified with him in order that the body of sin might be brought to nothing, so that we would no longer be enslaved to sin. For one who has died has been set free from sin." I believed the bonds of sin were stronger than the power of grace. Naturally, I turned to performance, not grace. At every failure, I concluded that I needed to work harder, get better accountability, and perhaps find a stronger discipler. What I did not know is that discipleship is not performance based. What I needed is what all of us need—continual belief in the depth of God's forgiveness and the resilience of his genuine approval in Christ. In brief, what I needed was more Jesus, not more discipline. As Bonhoeffer points out, I needed to give up on myself and give in to Jesus: "When a man really gives up trying to make something out of himself—a saint, or converted sinner, or a churchman, a righteous or unrighteous man, . . . when in the fullness of tasks, questions, success or ill-hap, experiences and perplexities, a man throws himself into the arms of God . . . then he wakes with Christ."[11]

We need to put performance and rebellion to sleep so that we can wake up to Jesus. The gospel promises us the arms of God's loving embrace every single minute of every single day, provided we give up on ourselves. When we give up on our rebellion and religion, we can give in to God's amazing grace. This surrender is a recentering of faith in Jesus. Jesus, alone, should take the center place in our lives, not our Bible reading, evangelism, character, or effort to be different or spiritual. No disciple will ever graduate from the school of grace. Every follower of Jesus needs to know, and be reminded, that the gospel that makes disciples is the very same gospel that matures disciples. We are born in grace and we breathe by grace, all bought by the blood of Jesus.

In summary, this gospel-centered definition of discipleship collapses the dichotomy between evangelism and discipleship by showing that disciples are made and matured through repentance and faith in the good news. If this news is what makes and matures a disciple, then evangelism and discipleship are both gospel endeavors. The gospel integrates, not dichotomizes, evangelism and discipleship by announcing a grace that saves and sanctifies disciples! Michael Horton captures this well when he writes: "We have to reevaluate the common assumption today that we move from being *evangelized* to being *discipled*. These terms are interchangeable. Believers need to be immersed in the gospel every week."[12]

This gospelcentric approach to disciple making is largely

missing from discipleship today, which tends to focus on evangelistic techniques and discipleship methods. Unless these methods are tethered to a robust understanding of the gospel, they will actually sabotage discipleship. What we need is a recentering of Christian discipleship. The Gospel Commission is not evangelism or discipleship centered; it is gospel centered. It calls us to make disciples by being a people who orbit around Jesus and his blood-bought benefits, not performance and self-made efforts. Disciples are gospel people who introduce and reintroduce themselves and others to the person and power of Jesus over and over again. A disciple of Jesus never stops learning the gospel, relating in the gospel, and communicating the gospel.

Integrated Discipleship

With a clear definition of "disciple" in place, we see that the gospel integrates, not dichotomizes, evangelism and discipleship. The key to resolving this dichotomy is the gospel itself. Before concluding our definition of discipleship, I will briefly sketch a more constructive, gospel-centered framework for discipleship. Jesus is the integrating center of everything!

The Integrating Gospel

When discipleship is gospel centered, it integrates more than evangelism and discipleship; it integrates all three aspects of a disciple through faith in Jesus Christ as Lord. Jesus uniquely brings the rational, relational, and missional aspects together as our Lord and Christ.

When the word *Lord* is used to refer to Jesus in the New Testament, it aligns Jesus with Yahweh.[13] Here's how: the Greek word for Lord, *kurios*, is used to refer to Yahweh in the

Greek version of the Old Testament (the Septuagint) *and* to Jesus in the Greek New Testament.[14] This is why: in the Old Testament, we see Yahweh referred to as Lord, and in the New Testament, we see Jesus referred to as Lord. This alignment places Jesus in God, where the Father and the Son share their identity and sovereignty. As part of the Godhead (together with the Spirit), they rule over all created things.[15] Therefore, when we read, "Jesus is Lord," divine identity and sovereignty should ripple through our minds in awe-inspiring recognition of an immense Jesus. To put this in simple terms, when we see Jesus referred to as Lord, we should see Jesus as *God* and Jesus as *King*.

Think, for a moment, about the implications of Jesus's divine lordship. If Jesus is *Lord*, then he doesn't merely rescue sinners from judgment, but he also brings disciples under his divine authority. Translation: when we become Jesus's disciples, we also become his *servants*.[16] Disciples are servants who take up their cross and follow him (Luke 9:23).[17] When we turn to Jesus, we turn everything over to him. When we confess Jesus as Lord, we embrace his authority over every aspect of our lives. This is precisely why Bonhoeffer can say: "When Jesus calls a man, he bids him to come and die."[18] When Jesus is Lord, we give up on our old life (a sort of death) in order to live a new life. When we put our faith in Jesus as Lord, we surrender self-rule in order to come under God's wise, gracious, and all-powerful rule. We submit to his reign and join his mission. This life-altering truth forms Jesus's preface to the Gospel Commission: "All authority in heaven and on earth has been given to me" (Matt. 28:18). This new, expansive, awe-inspiring authority orders the life of a disciple to learn the gospel, relate in the gospel, and communicate the gospel in glad submission to King Jesus. As a result, we grow in the gospel as his servants, relate in the gospel as part of his family, and communicate the gospel as his ambassador-missionaries. As Lord, Jesus integrates the rational, relational, and missional aspects of discipleship under his sovereign and divine authority. Consequently, wherever we go, the King goes, and where the King goes, people will bow.[19]

But what happens when we fail under Jesus's lordship? How does King Jesus respond to disloyal servants who go headlong into sin? We discover Jesus as *Christ*. The Greek word for Christ is *Christos*, which means "anointed one." This title refers to Jesus's messianic identity as the anointed servant of the Lord, prophesied by Isaiah, as the one who would rescue and redeem God's people (Isaiah 42, 49, 50, 53). Jesus rescues and forgives disloyal, undeserving disciples from their sin over and over again through his once-for-all death on the cross. The King becomes Servant for all who hope in him, when Jesus lays his life down to atone for our every failure to obey and honor him as Lord. The King descends from his throne, moves out beyond the courtyard to a place outside the city, where his body is engulfed in sin to sanctify a people for himself: "So Jesus also suffered outside the gate in order to sanctify the people through his own blood" (Heb. 13:12). God made the one who did not know sin to be sin for us, "so that in him we might become the righteousness God" (2 Cor. 5:21). Because Jesus is not only Lord but also Christ, every disciple has every reason to hope in failure. Jesus has secured our never-ending forgiveness through the end of his life. And with his triumph over death, he bought for us a new life of glad submission to him. Because Jesus is Christ, he is sufficient for our failures and strong for our successes.

When disciples turn to Jesus Christ as Lord, they gain a

whole new way of living under God's reign in his grace. Jesus is King and Jesus is Savior. God has made Jesus "both Lord and Christ" so that he might make and multiply a new humanity after the image of his glorious Son (Acts 2:36). Therefore, when a gospel as lofty as Jesus's lordship and as earthy as his suffering take center place in the heart and life of a disciple, the impact is immeasurable. This good news can affect *everything* in our lives as we rest in Christ and live for the Lord.

Vertical Discipleship

When Jesus is Lord of everything, it can be difficult to focus on something. Some disciples focus on piety, a category that includes spiritual disciplines and personal holiness. Others prefer to focus on mission, a category that includes social justice, evangelism, and cultural renewal. Gospel-centered discipleship radically alters our approach to both Christian piety and mission. Very often, pious disciples and missional disciples don't mix. Pious disciples tend to withdraw from the world (to draw near to God), while missional disciples tend to engage the world (to bring God near to it).

The differences between these foci run deeper than preference. It is a division that springs from a foundational crack in our understanding of discipleship. As the crack grows, it sends Christians in one of two ways of being a disciple. The first way, piety-centered discipleship, is associated with our personal relationship with God. We will call this *vertical discipleship*. Vertical discipleship points up to God's character, showing us how great he is and how far we fall short. Vertical discipleship promises to close the gap between our sin and God's holiness through things like Bible reading, prayer, fasting, confession, and personal piety in order to know God. Entire branches of Christianity, such as monasticism, have focused on this vertical aspect of discipleship. When Jesus is simply Lord over our piety, disciples begin to measure their Christianity in ways that run counter to the gospel. Vertical disciples unknowingly try to cultivate righteousness on their own apart from Christ. You may have this tendency if you get down on yourself for not reading the Bible enough or for having a weak prayer life. The implication here is that you are "up on yourself" if you do read the Bible more and have a strong prayer life. Piety-centered discipleship says: "Be this kind of person and you can feel good about yourself." The gospel, however, says: "Give up on yourself and become the person you already are in Christ."

Unfortunately, piety often isolates us from mission, quarantining the disciple from Jesus's expansive lordship. Ironically, the "pious" disciple in pursuit of God ends up with an incomplete God, subtracting mission from the missionary God. In an attempt to withdraw and know God, they fail to know his whole character. As a young disciple, I vehemently practiced vertical discipleship. I spent lots of time in prayer, fasting, study, and striving for holiness. I kept prayer journals, fasted regularly, memorized lots of Scripture, and pleaded with God to "break me" so that I could become holier. While God accomplished some great things in me during that season, piety-driven discipleship actually drove me away from grace.

Horizontal Discipleship

The second direction a disciple can go when Jesus is not both Lord and Christ is horizontal. If vertical discipleship points up to God's character, *horizontal discipleship* points out to God's mission. It focuses on missional activity such as evangelism, social justice, and cultural renewal. In horizontal discipleship, mission is easily divorced from piety. Strangely, it can become a substitute form of piety, an alternative self-made righteousness. The "missional" disciple discovers righteousness, not in who he is (holy), but in what he does (mission). He tends to separate God's mission from God, focusing on what he can do for God as a disciple. When sharing the gospel, feeding the poor, or making great culture, the "missional" disciple feels up; but when he fails to do these consistently or with results, he feels down. This emotional roller coaster isn't much fun. Believe me. Mission-centered discipleship has very little personal need for Christ. It also restricts his lordship to the horizontal way of living. Mission-centered discipleship says: "Do missional deeds and you can feel up." The gospel says: "Because Jesus completed the mission (Col. 1:20), you can give up on your deeds and give in to Christ."

Every disciple has a leaning, either toward the vertical or the horizontal. As I matured, I began to focus more on horizontal discipleship—spending more time doing world missions, evangelism, church planting, and social justice. When we lean toward the vertical *or* horizontal, we disintegrate discipleship. When integration is lacking, disciples easily become disillusioned and their character distorted. We can weary of the balancing act between piety and mission, as we swing back and forth between the two. In the midst of this disintegration, disciples sometimes give up, not realizing that what they gave up wasn't Christianity but a form of discipleship centered on the wrong thing. The good news is that Jesus hasn't called us to a life of balancing piety and mission. Instead, he has called us to a gospel-centered life that focuses in on Jesus as our Christ (forgiveness and righteousness) and as our Lord (King and Deliverer).

Diagonal Discipleship Is Integrated

Isn't it wonderful that we don't have to choose between vertical and horizontal discipleship? We do not have to run between the *X* and *Y* axis of piety and mission, keeping record of our pious and missional success in order to impress the Father. The gospel actually integrates piety and mission around a new gospel center. When the gospel is central to discipleship, our acceptance before God isn't performance based but grace based. The gospel frees us from running ragged trying to please God with holiness and social justice, because Jesus has pleased God for us and secured the mission. Jesus is telling us to give up on our deeds and ourselves, and to give in to his deeds and him—as our Christ and as our Lord. The gospel frees us to rest in Christ and to live for the Lord neither vertically nor horizontally, but *diagonally*.

Integrated Discipleship

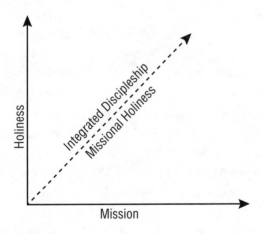

Integrated Discipleship

A diagonal disciple lives by faith in Jesus Christ as Lord, not by faith in piety or mission. He or she recognizes that being a disciple is not primarily about having a personal relationship with Jesus, or joining a missional church. Instead, a diagonal disciple relates primarily to Jesus Christ as Lord, who graciously rules over the whole of life, not just one aspect of it. His expansive lordship prohibits division between piety and mission because Jesus reigns over every sphere of life. The Colossian hymn (1:15–20) shows us, in staggering theology, that Jesus is Lord of creation and redemption. All things were made in, through, and for him. Similarly, all things are reconciled in, through, and for him. He holds all things together as the agent of creation and redemption. Therefore, *Jesus* is what keeps created things and redeemed things from falling apart. As Creator, he is concerned with the whole realm of mission—his creation. As Redeemer, he has accomplished the reconciliation of impious men (Col. 1:21). Jesus, then, is the lynchpin of creation and redemption, holding mission and piety together as Lord and Christ! This means that Jesus has to be central, not piety or mission, or discipleship will fall apart, disintegrate, and disappoint. The gospel reminds us that Jesus is central, and as we believe its good news, we discover discipleship integrates and interweaves us deeply into his life. In his lordship we perceive that all things exist in, through, and for him (Col. 1:15–23), making all of life a matter of devotion to him (Col. 3:23–24), not to pious or missional performance.

Consequently, the gospel-centered disciple serves Jesus at work and at home, in the study and in the projects, in church and in culture. His aim is public obedience of every kind. He does this, not for approval, but from resilient approval in Christ Jesus. The gospel frees us to follow Jesus without fear of moral or missional failure. Jesus stands as the great King over every aspect of a disciple's life, requiring devotion to him that, in turn, fosters a life of both piety and mission. And when we fail in our devotion to him as our Lord, he remains our Christ, the Messiah who bears our sin and grants us forgiveness. Jesus remains central, whether it is through obedience or repentance. As a result, the death, resurrection, and continuing reign of Jesus Christ form the integrating center of discipleship. Jesus Christ is Lord, and when he is, all of life becomes a theater of devotion to him.

I failed to grasp this essential gospel (Jesus as Lord) as a young disciple. Even today I drift from the center, placing my faith in my vertical (holiness) or horizontal (missional performance). But I now understand that Jesus is still Christ in my wanderings, and that his grace brings me back to faith in him. He's not measuring my performance; he's just asking me to trust him. When I do, he puts my heart back together, removes my shame, and orders my loves. A diagonal disciple lives an integrated life by faith in Jesus Christ as Lord. We trust Jesus as Savior and serve Jesus as King. This staggering view of Jesus compels holiness and mission. He is grander and deeper than we thought. As we continually come back to him, we increasingly long for him to be revealed as the Lord of all. We fight to trust and obey him out of devotion, not mere duty. As a result, gospel-centered disciples refuse to focus on piety and mission but assiduously hone in on Jesus Christ our Lord. We cease to pit the vertical against the horizontal in view of who Jesus really is, and as a result, we live as disciples devoted to God and to his mission.[20] We become integrated disciples who choose a whole way of life living wholly under the gracious lordship of King Jesus.

In summary, the biblical definition of a disciple is radically Jesus centered. It brings all three aspects of a disciple (rational, relational, missional) together in the gospel, which show us a whole way of living wholly by faith in Jesus Christ as Lord.

We learn the gospel, relate in the gospel, and communicate the gospel in everyday life. It is central in everything, from the way we relate to God to the way we relate to others. Of course, just because the gospel integrates our lives in Christ and under his lordship does not mean we cease to struggle. In fact, sin wants to disintegrate and unravel us from belief in the gospel, spinning us away from Jesus in any other possible direction. This is why the Bible constantly calls disciples to fight for belief in the gospel.

2

THE GOAL OF DISCIPLESHIP: FIGHTING FOR IMAGE

Everyone fights for goals. Moms fight for their kids to feel loved. Athletes train hard to break records and win titles. Salespeople work long hours to make the sale. Goals motivate. Similarly, if a disciple's goal is worthwhile, we will fight to reach it. This chapter will identify the goal of discipleship and how to obtain it. As the goal of discipleship comes into focus, it will be important to know what kind of fighting to employ. The word *fight* calls to mind a variety of images.

Fighting cuts across both genders. In general, men like a fight. They tend to think of physical combat, perhaps a high school fight, ultimate fighting, or movies like *Rocky*. More than ever, fighting imagery collects around digital media.

According to a recent statistic, the online gaming industry exceeded movie rentals in 2009. Virtual fighting is among game favorites. The overnight success of games like the World of Warcraft and Grand Theft Auto demonstrate that our desire for a fight is far from gone. In a game called Deadspace, the goal is not merely killing but dismemberment. Consider www.666games.net, a website entirely devoted to violent games like Whack Your Boss, The Torture Game 2, and Orchestrated Death. The 666 Games tagline reads: "Welcome to 666 *Games*, we serve you the most violent, brutal, sadistic and bloody flash games on the Internet. *Always keep in mind it's just digital violence*" (emphasis not added). Is this the kind of combat men have been created for? Killing our digital bosses, torturing virtual people, and orchestrating death? Is our fighting pointed in the right direction? Josh Jackson, editor of *Paste* magazine, cautions our unthinking participation in violent media:

> Violence in the media is a terrible thing. Except of course, for those great battle scenes in The Lord of the Rings. . . . I am really repulsed by the idea of torture-porn flicks like Saw and Hostel, and don't understand how anyone could enjoy watching them. And I'm bothered by games like Grand Theft Auto that put you in the shoes of a gangster. Yet I gleefully watch Samuel L. Jackson burst onto the scene like the vengeful hand of God and lay waste to pathetic junkies in Pulp Fiction. . . . From the Bible to the work of Cormac McCarthy, the best stories are filled with conflict, and often that takes the form of violent antagonists and heroes who fight for justice.[1]

What sets biblical fighting apart from digital fighting? One distinctive is that biblical fighting calls us to fight for a noble cause—justice, for instance. Alternatively, digital fighting calls us to fight for entertainment. At best, virtual fighting procures a fictional justice. At worst, it functions as a kind of voyeurism, a medium through which men escape the responsibilities of real manhood for the rush of irresponsible entertainment. Men who have nothing to fight for in real life live out their fighting desires through the video screen. This voyeurism isn't remotely manly, but it does reveal the innate, sometimes suppressed desire to fight for something worthwhile. Deep down, men long for a noble fight.

Women also fight. They generally fight to be unique, recognized, or beautiful. At best, this kind of fighting reveals a longing to be noticed and loved. At worst, this fighting is a competition between women in fashion, beauty, and influence. Competitive beauty makes self the center of attention. Being noticed isn't inherently bad,[2] but when the desire to be noticed, appreciated, and adored is so strong that it causes you to compete against other women, it distorts femininity. It is difficult to be content with our appearance because we receive a thousand messages a day that tell us to improve our beauty. This reminds me of the Oakley sunglasses advertisement that shows supermodel, Karena Dawn, running with a pair of $130 shades on. The billboard reads: "Perform beautifully." The sign says it all. True beauty is a competition. You are up against supermodels and airbrushed women. So take all the help you can get, even if it includes running with $130 shades when you can only afford $10. The principle driving this kind of beauty is a principle of *performance*. Perform well against one another and you will gain the title of beautiful; you will get the attention of others. Perform poorly, and you fail to be beautiful and fail to be noticed. This is a great lie from the pit of marketing hell. True beauty is not a competition based on performance. In fact, competition actually distorts beauty around a false notion of feminine identity. What women need to fight for is true beauty.

So you see, everyone fights for something. The desire to fight isn't masculine or feminine; it is human. Deep down we all want to be noticed, for our lives to count for something. We want to be beautiful or noble. The problem is that we direct our fighting desires toward the wrong things. We work hard at being noticed or entertained. We fall short of beauty and nobility. What would happen if, instead of spending hours in front of the video screen or mirror, we spent hours in front of the gospel? What if we fought for a more noble cause, a more beautiful image?

Fighting for Image

As a wayward college student, I needed a cause more noble than piety and a beauty more breathtaking than any woman could offer. I needed to fight for the nobility of faith in Jesus Christ as Lord and to be ravished with the image of his glory shining in the face of Jesus Christ (2 Cor. 4:6). Although I was unaware of it, I was fighting for an image that was far from noble and breathtaking.

We are all concerned about our images. Hipsters work hard to look like they don't care about image. Professionals work equally hard to look like they do care about image. We all project our values through the way we present ourselves. In writing this book, I am tempted to make writing decisions that reflect an intellectual image, instead of writing in a way that will best serve you. We all face the temptation to project false images of ourselves because we find the real image inadequate. This is easily done with social media. Our online image is often different from our offline image. With our Facebook status, we can project how we want others to see us, not who we truly are. Blog posts can be shrouded in airs of intellectualism, edginess, or humility. If we are honest, our real image is nowhere near as attractive as we want it to be. We want to be more beautiful, more successful, more creative, more virtuous, more popular, and more intelligent than we actually are. We all have an image problem. The problem, however, is not that we lack beauty, success, creativity, virtue, popularity, or intelligence. The problem is that we believe the lie that says that obtaining those images will actually make us happy. Believing the lie, we fight rigorously to obtain (or retain) our images of choice.

We discipline ourselves to lose weight, or climb the vocational ladder, learn new techniques, make moral decisions, or strive to be in the know, all to gain the images we so desperately want. We fight and scrap to obtain our desired perception. Why? Because we believe that being perceived a certain way will make us truly happy. We fight with whatever it takes—money, time, sacrifice, overworking, and the occasional white lie. In doing so, we believe a lie. We express faith in what is false. We rely on the unreliable. Only after we realize our tendency to build our identity on things that are untrue and unreliable can we begin to sink our identity into what is truly reliable. Nobility and beauty travel along the lines of truth. If none of the images above truly satisfy, what kind of image should we be striving for? What offers true beauty and a truly noble cause?

The Image of God

Christianity is about image. It affirms that we were created in God's image (Gen. 1:26–28), disfigured in our fall with Adam (Rom. 5:12–21), and are in desperate need of renewal. This image constitutes our essential dignity as human beings. It is an imprint of the Creator's divine nature, which includes our ability to rule and relate. Apart from the redeeming work of God to restore our image, we rule and relate in very distorted ways. We rule over instead of for one another, and we relate out of a distorted sense of what will truly make us happy. As a result, we treat God and others with contempt and disregard. The good news is that God wants to restore our image in Christ (2 Cor. 3:18; Col. 3:10). He promises a restored image in Jesus, who is the image of the invisible God (Col. 1:15). He holds up the image of Jesus as most glorious, and through the gospel, opens our eyes to his never-ending beauty (2 Cor. 4:6). Only by looking to Jesus can our disfigured image be restored and our contemptuous disregard forgiven. When we look away from ourselves and into the face of Christ, we behold "the light of the knowledge of the glory of God in the face of Jesus Christ" (2 Cor. 4:6). This gospel knowledge corrects our vision so that we not only behold but also become the image of the glory of God in Christ. True nobility and beauty converge in the image of Jesus.

It is a fundamental truth that we become what we behold.[3] Children become like their parents; interns become like their mentors. If we behold the beauty of Christ, we become beautiful like Christ. While it is true that our first glance into the face of Christ restores our image (Rom. 5:1–2; 8:29–30), it is also true that we drift back into fashioning our own distorted image. We slip into our own distorted forms of masculinity and femininity. The gospel calls us back to look at Jesus over and over again. A disciple of Jesus is a person who so looks at Jesus that he or she actually begins to reflect his beauty in everyday life. The gospel gives us the eyes to see Jesus as well as the power to look like him. It changes us into the image of his glory: "And we all, with unveiled face, beholding the glory of the Lord, are being transformed into the same image from one degree of glory to another" (2 Cor. 3:18). This transformative vision comes from the presence and power of the Holy Spirit (2 Cor. 3:17–18), who we will discuss at length in chapter 5. For now, suffice it to say that gospel-centered disciples rely on the Spirit, who focuses our hearts' attention on Jesus, where beholding him results in becoming like him. This is a goal worth fighting for.

The gospel also offers the hope of final transformation. One day our dusty image of Adam will be transformed entirely into the heavenly image of Christ: "Just as we have borne the image of the man of dust, we shall also bear the image of the man of heaven" (1 Cor. 15:49). This transformation, however, does not come without a struggle. Any image takes hard work, and in the words of J. P. Moreland, "Grace is opposed to earning, not to effort."[4] If we are to enjoy the breathtaking beauty of Jesus, we must put effort into the noble fight of faith.

The Fight of Faith

We have observed that everyone fights for an image, but not all images are equal. The image of Christ is far superior to anything else in its nobility and beauty. Therefore, it is worth the fight. Alternative images will eventually fail us, but the image of the glory of God shining out of Jesus's face will not. Goodness, thinking about this makes me want to so fight for faith in the gospel that God's glory bursts right through me. What, then, does it look like to fight for the image of Christ?

The fighting imagery used in the New Testament varies. Sometimes the imagery is associated with warfare, "wage the good warfare" (1 Tim. 1:18; 2 Cor. 10:3–4). Other times it draws on athletic or boxing imagery: "Fight the good fight of the faith" (1 Tim. 6:12). Both of the original Greek words in these verses tap into imagery associated with a kind of fight. The primary word for *fight* in the New Testament is *agonizo*, from which we get the word *agonize*. It means "to contend, struggle with difficulties and dangers antagonistic to the gospel."[5] Paul uses *agonizo* throughout his letters to communicate the struggle associated with believing the gospel (1 Cor. 9:25; Col. 1:29, 4:12; 1 Tim. 4:10; 6:12; 2 Tim. 4:7). Biblical fighting, then, is a spiritual contending to believe the truth of the gospel. This contending is reflected in Paul's repeated reminders to Timothy to fight for faith in the gospel:

- "*Fight the good fight of the faith.* Take hold of the eternal life to which you were called and about which you made the good confession in the presence of many witnesses." (1 Tim. 6:12)
- "This command I entrust to you, Timothy, my son . . . you *fight the good fight,* keeping faith and a good conscience." (1 Tim. 1:18–19 NASB)
- "I have *fought the good fight,* I have finished the race, I have kept the faith." (2 Tim. 4:7)

Like Timothy, we have been called to "take hold" of eternal life. There is urgency to our faith. True faith struggles to pry our hands off the old life and keep them on our eternal life. Biblical faith fights to believe the gospel to such a degree that it is reflected in our practice. Disciples fight to believe *that Jesus's death and resurrection is our death and resurrection.* His death is our death and his life our life (Romans 5; Galatians 2). As a result, the lie-believing, image-distorting life is dead, and in its place we have received a truth-believing, Christ-adoring life (Eph. 4:20–24). However, because of our tendency to return to the old image, we walk by faith until we see Jesus, when faith will correspond with sight (2 Cor. 5:6–7; Gal. 2:20). Until then, we fight, contend, and struggle. Believing the gospel is not a passive, one-time decision; it is an active, continual fight for faith in what God says is noble, true, and good.

Refusing to fight has devastating consequences. Think of a fight where one person refuses to attack. The opponent disfigures the reluctant fighter. Paul reminds us that surrendering the fight wrecks us: "This command I entrust to you, Timothy, my son . . . you fight the good fight, keeping faith and a good conscience, which some have rejected and suffered shipwreck in regard to their faith. Among these are Hymenaeus and Alexander, whom I have handed over to Satan, so that they will be taught not to blaspheme" (1 Tim. 1:18–20 NASB). If we cease to struggle, we can end up in the hands of Satan.[6] The fight matters.

Real faith is fighting faith. Once the fight begins, we must never stop fighting. We must "not lose heart" (2 Cor. 4:1, 16) in this great and glorious struggle. Gospel transformation comes through pain, struggle, suffering, and staring your ugly sin right in the face. The trick is to stare it down with truth. Nobody sins because they want to be deceived. We sin because we believe what sin offers is true. We believe that being sexually aroused will bring us personal satisfaction or being socially in the know will bring us meaningful acceptance. So, we look at porn and gossip about others. If we really believed that porn and gossip were based on lies that don't satisfy, we wouldn't participate in them.

Sin lies to us. We need to get in the habit of talking back with the truth. Instead of expressing faith in the lies of sin, we need to have faith in the truth of the gospel. The gospel is "the light of the knowledge of the glory of God in the face of Jesus Christ" (2 Cor. 4:6). It is the heartwarming, mind-renewing truth that the image of the glory of God in the complexion of Jesus is all we need to be truly satisfied, complete, and accepted. We receive it by faith, over and over again. When we labor to look at Jesus, we begin to look like him, to be transformed into his image. This is why the fight of faith is so important. It is based on the truth and it truly changes us. Although the fight of faith is humbling and hard, it is worth it. It is a good and glorious fight.

In summary, disciples of Jesus are called to fight, not in physical or virtual combat, but for the noble cause of everyday faith in Jesus. We are called to beauty, not through performance, but by beholding Jesus. We fight to behold the image of the glory of God shining in the face of Jesus Christ. This faith fights not for perfection, but for belief. We fight to believe that Jesus is more precious, satisfying, and thrilling than anything else this world has to offer. This is faith in the gospel—the grand announcement that Jesus has defeated sin, death, and evil through his own death and resurrection and is making all things new, even us. When we believe the gospel, we get to enjoy the promises of God's grace, peace, and joy. When we don't believe the gospel, we move away from these things. Most of all, we move away from Jesus, who is worth our every effort, every gaze, and every belief.

PART TWO

Getting to the Heart

3

TWISTED MOTIVES:
THE FAILURE OF DISCIPLESHIP

There are many things worth contending for, especially as Christians. Our churches should be filled with fighting—fighting for justice, for peace, for holiness, for perseverance, for faith, for one another, and for the gospel. The problem is that many of us don't fight, or we fight for the wrong things. To be frank, some Christians fight like cowards, backing out of the fight of faith. Others fight like bullies, beating up themselves or others. Everyone tends toward one direction or the other. Whether we lean into or away from fighting, we do so for particular reasons. Our response is dictated by our motives, which can be easily twisted. In this chapter, we will consider two ways our motivations are twisted away from the gospel.

The Failure of Accountability[1]

Christians who punish one another with the Word of God are often applauded. Think of the person who is quick to quote (not counsel) Scripture whenever someone shares a sin or struggle. The religious person insensitively admonishes others to obey God's Word without extending God's grace. The religious thrive in accountability relationships or accountability groups. Christian accountability typically tries to foster obedience to Christ by "holding a person accountable" to a checklist of godly virtues. Accountability partners will gather together to ask questions of one another which are often stated in the negative, for example: "Have you exposed yourself to any sexually explicit material?" "Have any of your financial dealings lacked integrity?" The questions asked lift up good, godly rules like sexual purity and financial integrity. However, the questions tend to focus on *not committing sin* as opposed *to cultivating virtue*. Very often these accountability lists conclude with a final question that goes something like: "Have you lied in any of the questions above?" Again, a negative statement is used to promote positive behavior. The emphasis is on adherence to (good) rules. This plays right into the hands of the legalist, who presses others with negative questions, interrogating their morality in order to promote "holiness." Those who don't like the rules, the rebellious, avoid this kind accountability or simply hope the questions won't be asked!

Although accountable relationships start with a noble aim—commitment to confession, encouragement, and prayer for one another—they often devolve into relationships based on rule keeping or rule breaking. The religious verbally punish others for failing to keep the rules, while the rebellious are quick to overlook one another's failure. Both are rule centered. The religious person is oriented around keeping rules, and the rebellious person around breaking rules. Whether you've experienced "accountability groups" or not, we all experience the impulse to either keep or break rules.

Religious Accountability

After I got back on a moral track in college, I leaned upon accountable relationships to stay on track. I placed too much faith in accountability and not enough faith in the gospel. Then I began discipling others with this rule-keeping bent. When I recall the discipleship I advocated, I shudder. When one of the guys I was discipling caved in to a particular sin he was "being held accountable for," he had to put ten bucks in a jar. I enforced the punishment for breaking the moral rules. In our aim to promote holiness, ten bucks was the penalty for pandering to sin. We thought this approach to accountability was especially good for fighting sexual sin. If one of the guys I discipled had a particularly lustful week (viewing inappropriate TV, reading pornographic material, or masturbating), he had to "pay the price." When we met for our weekly accountability meeting, I would ask a range of questions designed to promote accountability, but as I recall, we only assigned sexual sins the steep penalty of ten dollars. Other sins were considered less grievous. Sometimes the accumulated cash was put in the offering, other times it was used to celebrate "not sinning" over dinner. Somehow, this practice was supposed to motivate holy living, but instead, it fostered a religious legalism that undercut a more biblical approach to fighting sin.

In legalistic accountability groups, failures to perform are punished through graduated penalties (an increased tithe, buying lunch or coffee for the partners, or unspoken ostracism from one's peers). Instead of holding one another accountable to belief in the gospel, we become accountable for exacting punishments. The unfortunate result is a kind of legalism in which peer-prescribed punishments are substitutes for repentance and faith in Jesus. As a result, our motives for holiness get twisted. Confession in such contexts is relegated to "keeping from sinning," making discipleship a duty-driven, rule-keeping journey. We end up fighting against the church instead of with her.

Confessional-Booth Accountability

Alternatively, accountable relationships can devolve into a kind of confessional booth. I confess my sin; you confess yours. I pat your back. You pat mine. Then we pray. We depart absolved of any guilt, fearing merely the passing frown of our fellow confessor. Accountability groups become circles of cheap grace, through which we obtain cheap peace from a troubled conscience. Confession is divorced from repentance, reducing holiness to half-hearted morality. Accountability becomes a man-made mix of spineless confession and cheap peace. This approach to discipleship is hollow. It lacks the urgency required by the fight of faith and, consequently, loses sight of the all-important goal of the image of Christ. This kind of Christianity will dry up in a matter of time if it does not develop deep roots into the gospel of grace. I have watched confessional-booth Christians slowly drift away from Christ in the name of "Christian freedom." Surely there is a better way to follow Jesus.

True Confession

Those who avoid confession surrender the fight. This unfortunate surrender leads to sick disciples who hobble along in unbelief, refusing to believe God's promise of healing in confession: "Therefore, confess your sins to one another and pray for one another, that you may be healed" (James 5:16). When we avoid confession and prayer, we don't think of ourselves as cowardly or indifferent to grace. In fact, when we lack an earnest faith, we don't always appear sick. We may seem very normal, cordial with others, regular in church attendance, even fun to be around. But like an undiagnosed cancer patient, we carry on everyday life ignorant of the deadly disease growing inside of us—unconfessed sin. In Psalm 32:3–4, David poignantly describes the effect of unconfessed sin:

> For when I kept silent, my bones wasted away
>> through my groaning all day long.
> For day and night your hand was heavy upon me;
>> my strength was dried up as by the heat of summer.

We waste away when sin goes unconfessed and our hearts remain unrepentant. David was conscious of his unconfessed sin, but unfortunately, many of us are unaware of the strength-sapping effect of our unconfessed sin. We can become so passive in fighting the fight of faith that confession to others, and daily confession to God, seems bizarre. We might write off confession as morbid, failing to believe the way God has written it into our DNA, as a blessing. David discovers this blessing in the very same psalm:

> Blessed is the one whose transgression is forgiven,
>> whose sin is covered.
> Blessed is the man against whom the LORD counts no iniquity,
>> and in whose spirit there is no deceit. (Ps. 32:1–2)

The person without deceit is a person who is honest about who he or she is—failures and all. Honest confession brings the blessing of forgiveness, and forgiveness brings us back under God's blessing to enjoy his grace and peace. The goal in confession isn't to cleanse ourselves before God, because we can't (Zech. 3:3–5; Ps. 51:1–2; 1 John 1:7). And it isn't to forgive ourselves because our sin isn't ultimately against self; it's against God (Gen. 39:9; Ps. 51:4).[2] God is the standard of righteousness and the judge of sinfulness. Fortunately, God is not only judge but also Redeemer to us in Jesus. In fact, Jesus quotes Psalm 32:2 to refer to Nathanael's unwavering hope in the Messiah, a Messiah who alone could climb the ladder between God's holiness and man's sinfulness to offer forgiveness to those who hope in him (John 1:47–51). This forgiveness is a fountain flowing from Jesus's side, available to all who are willing to reveal their dirty garments and dip them in his guilt-absorbing blood: "If we confess our sins, he is faithful and just to forgive us our sins and to cleanse us from all unrighteousness" (1 John 1:9). Upon the condition of confession, we receive God's forgiveness and cleansing. We return to Christ our righteousness, where we are perfectly loved and accepted.

Therefore, confession isn't to be viewed as a ritual bargaining chip we cash in to obtain a clear conscience. Our forgiveness has already been bought in Jesus; we simply procure his purchased forgiveness through confession. This may seem abstract. Perhaps it would be helpful to think of confession in terms of *authenticity*. Confession is a verbal way of spiritually recovering our authenticity in Christ. Confession rejects an inauthentic image in order to realign with our true image. Sin stands in the way of authenticity. It is a silent, spiritual rejection of our identity in Christ. It denies judgment and grace. However, when we confess our sin in true repentance, we come to our senses in Jesus. We return to ourselves. Confession of sin is a kind of repentance from being inauthentic. It's as if we say: "Heavenly Father, forgive me for not acting like your child, for pretending to be someone I'm not. I want to return to my authentic self as your beloved child and live accordingly." Confession relies on Christ's judgment and grace. He bears our judgment (for sin) and gives us his grace (as his children). The gospel reminds us to live authentically as his children, either through repentance or obedience. In confession, we become authentically Christian, agreeing with God about our judgment-deserving sin and trusting in his sin-forgiving grace. We return to the reality of grace, in Christ, which in turn compels real obedience.

Both the religious rule keeper and the confessionless rule breaker are inauthentic. They choose "sinner" over "son." The difference between the two is that the rebel avoids God while the religious person tries to impress him. One runs away from him, while the other runs past him. Instead, rebels and the religious need to run straight to God in confession of their sin and in confidence of his forgiveness. The reason we can confidently run to God is because we have an advocate in Christ. Jesus sits ready to receive us. Right now he sits at the right hand of the Father ready to plead our innocence: "But if anyone does sin, we have an advocate with the Father, Jesus Christ the righteous" (1 John 2:1). His advocacy never ceases: "He always lives to make intercession" for us (Heb. 7:25). In Jesus, we have an advocate with the Father who bore our judgment and pleads our innocence![3] As a result, we can be forgiven and accepted by a just and holy God. The gospel coaxes us to run neither away nor past God but straight into his loving arms. In the gospel, we get to live authentically as God's forgiven and accepted sons and daughters. Grace brings us to our senses, delivering us from the insanity of sin.

Rebellious and religious disciples don't make the gospel central in their motivation for following Jesus. Their twisted motives lead to inauthentic living. What we need are gospel motivations, which lead to authentic living. Before addressing gospel motivation in depth, let's try to understand our twisted motivations a little more.

Religious Performance

Every disciple leans toward the motivation of religious performance or spiritual license. Some vacillate between these two extremes. Religious performance motivates the religious person, while spiritual license motivates the rebellious. Understanding and repenting from our leaning can lead to tremendous freedom and joy.

Legalism is the tendency in the human heart to measure our worth by how well we perform. It likes to keep rules and is driven by performance. Religious performance operates on an assumption—*if I perform well, God will accept me.* This assumption is subtle. Religious disciples don't think of themselves as legalists. They aim for a spiritual image. They think of themselves as either pretty good or pretty bad Christians, depending on how well they perform that day. This is true of both vertical and horizontal discipleship. Religious performance can be expressed spiritually, missionally, or morally.

Christians from a pietistic background perform *spiritually* to impress God—regular Bible reading, prayer, fasting, speaking in tongues, and service. Christians oriented toward mission perform *missionally*—renewing their city, serving the poor, sharing the gospel, and making disciples. Other Christians perform *morally*—avoiding "the culture," doing what's right, exposing what is wrong. The trouble with this performance-driven discipleship is that it is awfully unreliable. If we perform well in our version of Christianity, we think highly of ourselves, but when we perform poorly we think poorly of ourselves. Our self-image rises and falls with our spiritual, missional, or moral performance. Like a nauseating roller coaster, discipleship by religious performance will seem fun at first, but it eventually leaves a bad taste in your mouth.

At different stages in my discipleship, piety and morality have been my preferred paths of performance. As I began to make disciples in college, I focused on piety. I was trying to get it right, and in a subtle way, make up for my failures. I was motivated by a mix of genuine love for God and a desire to "get it right" so I could enjoy God's favor. Almost two decades later, I face a very different religious performance. As a pastor of a missional church, one of the ways I try to gain favor before God is through missional performance. Not a week goes by without self-interrogation. "Have I shared the gospel enough?" "Am I spending enough time making disciples?" "Am I serving the poor enough?" On one hand, these questions can be good for me. They help me cultivate integrity and live in a way that blesses others. On the other hand, they can be a substitute form of acceptance before God. If I'm evangelizing, discipling, or serving consistently (and with results), then I'll feel more approved by God. This isn't living by faith in Jesus Christ as Lord; it's living by faith in a missional Jonathan Dodson. The legalist emphasizes piety or mission apart from faith in Jesus Christ as Lord. Holiness or social justice can become our functional lord. This is deadly. Whenever we replace Jesus with another lord, we displace the gospel from the center of our discipleship. We substitute Jesus's perfect performance for our imperfect performance, which will always fail. The gospel reminds us that our approval before God rests, not on our performance but on the performance of Jesus in his perfect life, death, and resurrection. Religious performance deceives us by saying: "Impress God and he will approve of you." The truth of the gospel, however, says: "You don't have to impress God because Jesus has impressed him for you."[4] When we turn to the God of the gospel, we can't help but serve him. We serve not to receive his love but because we have already received his love, and love will compel a man to do remarkable things.

Spiritual License

Alternatively, spiritual license is the tendency in the human heart to find meaning in freedom from rules. Disciples who operate on spiritual license perceive themselves as liberated, set free from the bondage of more conservative Christians. Instead of believing the lie of performance—*If I perform, God will accept me*—they believe the lie of license—*Because God has forgiven me, I'm free to disobey*. Liberated Christians possess a license to break the rules, to disobey God's Word. They see holiness as negotiable. These disciples don't think of themselves as disobedient; they think of themselves as free, liberated Christians.

Liberated Christians boast a spiritual license that says they are not bound to rules. This license may be expressed by drinking too much, watching inappropriate films, or refraining from Bible reading, all in the name of spiritual freedom. The subtle assumption here is that true freedom comes from the ability to not keep rules. However, when freedom is constructed against rules, it is a false sense of freedom. The lie of spiritual license is partially true. Because of the costly death of Christ, forgiveness has been purchased for our disobedience. Because judgment has fallen on Christ for our sin, we are free, but not as we might think. God's forgiveness frees us from *judgment*, not from *obedience*.

Everyone obeys some kind of law. We are all enslaved to something. Even the rebellious disciple is obedient, bound to obey his or her fleeting desires. Those fleeting desires are connected to other "gods." For example, the god of self limits Bible reading while allowing an unlimited stream of Internet reading. "Free" to read whatever they like, the liberated Christians allow unfiltered data to float through their hearts and minds without the redemptive lens of Scripture. Consider the god of alcohol. The god of alcohol rules over the "free" drunk, who obediently takes drink after drink in pursuit of pleasure or escape. Those who are motivated by spiritual license are actually ruled by the ultimate god of freedom. Freedom to not read the Bible or to drink in excess actually ends up hurting more than helping. Freedom is a deceptive master. So while disciples who operate on spiritual license may appear liberated, they are, in fact, bound to a false, self-injurious form of freedom. The god of freedom actually deceives us by creating the illusion of freedom. In the words of Ray LaMontagne: "*And freedom can be an empty cup from which everybody want to drink.*"[5] Spiritual "freedom" looks full and satisfying but eventually proves empty and bitter. Spiritual license will eventually leave you with a hangover. Anyone who has chased this so-called freedom for any length of time can testify to its eventual, gnawing emptiness.

A disciple motivated by spiritual license drinks from the empty cup of spiritual freedom. Gospel-centered disciples drink deeply from the cup of costly grace and fight to live lives of obedience to King Jesus. Faith in the gospel actually makes us slaves of Christ, who frees us from sin and graciously binds us to his side. At his side, we discover a better God and enjoy a more gracious Master. Spiritual license deceives us by saying: "Because God has forgiven me, I'm free to disobey." The truth of the gospel is: "Because God has forgiven me in Christ, I'm bound to obey."[6] The gospel points us to Jesus as Christ and as Lord. No one is truly free. The religious are bound to keeping rules, and the rebellious are bound to breaking rules. The gospel, however, tells us that we are bound, not to rules, but to Christ. We have been crucified with Christ, and he now lives in us (Gal. 2:20). In Christ we are liberated from sin and delivered into the arms of our Savior. The gospel steeps our hearts in a new motivation of grace, which neither flaunts disobedience nor feigns obedience.

Grace gives us a new identity, not a new set of rules. We all need grace. We all need to be continually awakened to the beauty and glory of Christ and the sufficiency of his grace, which will in turn compel Christ-beholding obedience.

Thankfully, my discipleship and accountability has improved with time. Over the years I've come to realize the shortcomings of religious performance and spiritual license. I don't want to be religious or rebellious, though I still succumb to both. What I want is a better image, a more noble cause, and a deeper satisfaction. I want Jesus Christ as my Lord. How can we make Jesus central and avoid these twisted motivations? We need to displace what is at the center of our discipleship. We need to remove rules, rule keeping (religion), and rule breaking (rebellion), from the center of discipleship and replace it with the gospel, which graciously binds us to Christ's side. Instead of forming relationships gathered around rules, we need to gather around Jesus.

4

GOSPEL MOTIVATION: THE CENTER OF DISCIPLESHIP

The role of gospel motivation in discipleship is frequently overlooked.[1] If religious performance and spiritual license are unbiblical motivations for discipleship, what do biblical motivations look like? How do we cultivate them?

The Motivational Center

Jesus incessantly emphasized the importance of motives: "The good person out of the good treasure of his heart produces good, and the evil person out of his evil treasure produces evil, for out of the abundance of the heart his mouth speaks" (Luke 6:45). Jesus taught his disciples not merely to do good, but that true goodness comes from the heart. Why the heart? In Jewish theology, the heart encompasses the mind, will, and emotion. It was the motivational center for human action (cf. Gen. 6:5; Deut. 6:5; 1 Sam. 12:20; Ps. 51:6; Prov. 4:23; Acts 16:14; Rom. 10:9; Heb. 4:12). As Jesus points out, our hearts are a treasure trove of motives, whether good or evil. Therefore, if we want to bear the good fruit of Christian discipleship, it follows that we must pay attention to our heart motivations. It is here, in our motives, where following Jesus really begins. Motives are actually more important than our actions. We can do something right for all the wrong reasons. What *motivates* Jesus's followers is what *makes* his disciples. What our hearts behold, we become.

If the heart is the seat of human motivation, and we are prone to twisted motives, it follows that we need a motivation more captivating and enduring than religious performance or spiritual license. The Bible brings us back to gospel motivation over and over again. How does the gospel motivate discipleship? The remainder of this chapter will focus on three overlapping areas of gospel motivation—religious affections, repentance and faith, and promises and warnings. Authors like John Piper and Tim Keller have written extensively on the topic of Christian motivation. Keller uses the language of motivation more explicitly, frequently referring to the role of the gospel in motivating obedience. Piper, on the other hand, emphasizes the role of joy or religious affections in motivating obedience to God. Both Keller and Piper have been significantly influenced by the writings of Jonathan Edwards. I, too, have benefited tremendously from Edwards, in large part because of Piper's influence. Therefore, much of what I will say about religious affections and the gospel will reflect the influence of these men.

Religious Affection

One can hardly hear the name Jonathan Edwards without thinking about his emphasis on "religious affections." Contrary to what it sounds like, religious affection has nothing to do with religious performance. Perhaps "Christian affection" would be a helpful modernization of the phrase. Nevertheless, religious affection is affection for Christ that results in obedience to Christ. To say it another way, religious affection is gospel-generated delight in God. This delight compels us to follow Jesus, not because we have to, but because we get to. Religious affections motivate obedience to Jesus as Lord, not out of religious duty, but out of a foundational *delight*. Edwards writes: "The first foundation of the delight a true saint has in God, is his own perfection; and the first foundation of the delight he has in Christ, in his own beauty; he appears in himself the chief among ten thousand, and altogether lovely."[2] The perfection of God and the beauty of Christ are meant to thrill our souls. A true disciple possesses foundational delight in Jesus that compels obedience. The Bible regularly appeals to delight as a motivation for obedience:

- "If you *love* me, you will keep my commandments." (John 14:15)
- "*Delight* yourself in the LORD, and he will give you the *desires* of your heart." (Ps. 37:4)
- "Because you did not serve the LORD your God with *joyfulness* and *gladness* of heart. . . . therefore you shall serve your enemies whom the LORD will send against you." (Deut. 28:47–48)
- "*Rejoice* in the Lord always; again I will say, Rejoice." (Phil. 4:4)
- "*Rejoice* always." (1 Thess. 5:16)

The Bible is filled with appeals to delight in the Lord. Very often these appeals are followed by an ethical command. In John 15, Jesus repeatedly tells disciples to obey him out of their *love* for him. This is not unusual. Spouses, for instance, often serve one another out of love. In Philippians and Thessalonians, Paul issues a variety of moral commands, while calling us to rejoice at all times. God-centered delight is the foundation of a godly life.

With a basic understanding of religious affection, let's consider how it motivates following Jesus. Jonathan Edwards's famous honey analogy helpfully illustrates the role of religious affections in motivating obedience. Edwards explains faith by comparing it to honey.[3] Allow me to summarize:

I can show you honey. You can marvel at its golden hue, the way it refracts light, and its viscosity. And I can tell you that it is sweet . . . and you can believe that it is sweet. But unless you have tasted it, you don't know it is sweet. Believing honey is sweet doesn't mean you really know it is sweet. I could be lying to you. You only know honey is sweet when you have tasted it.

Similarly, faith does not merely believe Jesus but "tastes" *Jesus*. When we truly taste Jesus, we can't help but follow him. We move from mere belief into true faith, from notionally believing he is good to knowing he is good: "Taste and see that the LORD is good!" (Ps. 34:8). Tasting Christ is not getting whipped up into an emotional frenzy. It is a *genuine affection*, a sincere adoration of God that changes our behavior. Gospel-centered disciples are motivated by holy affection for God.

Religious affection is impossible apart from the gospel. The reason for this is that all men are born with animosity toward God (Ps. 51:5; Rom. 1:18–31). However, the gospel announces Jesus's victory over our sinful animosity through his death, and accomplishes our joyful surrender with his life. When we turn to Jesus, our hostile man is executed and a joyful man is born. *Through faith in the gospel, Jesus's death and resurrection become our death and resurrection.* We are buried in his death and raised into newness of life (Rom. 6:4). This is the good news—that Jesus has defeated sin, death, and evil, through his own death and resurrection, and is making all things new, even us. Such a gracious act liberates us from shallow joys to deliver us into infinite joy: "In [his] presence there is fullness of joy; at [his] right hand are pleasures forevermore" (Ps. 16:11). The gospel changes our motivations; it is an altering of joy. In Christ, we secure a new heart, capable of untold, and altogether superior, joy. Religious affection, then, is a gospel motivation because it is a new taste for God that arises from his work of new creation. Affectionate faith in Jesus is the gift of the gospel. This affection gives us strength for the fight of faith. We possess the strength to deny sinful pleasures because of our delight in a superior pleasure. Our draw toward discipleship is a draw toward the Master. Gospel-motivated disciples seek to obey God because it makes them truly happy.

Does this motivation sound too good to be true? Obey God because it makes you happy? John Piper points out that our joy and God's glory are not at odds when he states: "God is most glorified in us when we are most satisfied in Him."[4] He explains that our aim to be satisfied and God's aim to be glorified are not mutually exclusive. They are, in fact, intimately related. When we take pleasure in God, we confer honor on him. If he were to ask us: "Why did you obey me?" an appropriate response would be: "Because it was my pleasure." Every time I order from Chick-fil-A and express gratitude for my order, an employee inevitably says: "It's my pleasure." It's not unusual to hear an employee say this three or four times during a visit to Chick-fil-A! This has become a joke around our house, as we repeat the phrase over and over again with varying pitches: "It's my pleeeeasure!" What are they getting at? Do we really go to Chick-fil-A to make their employees happy? Not exactly. Then why do they repeat this phrase over and over again? Employees do this because they know that expressing pleasure in serving customers is a way to honor them. If they are delighted to serve us, this says we are worth serving. When we take pleasure in people, we demonstrate their value and worth. Whomever you take pleasure in most is the person you honor the most—your boyfriend/girlfriend, spouse, friend, or boss. Whomever you love most is your lord. This is especially true of God. He is the Person most deserving of our affection. When we serve God out of delight, we confer honor on him. God is glorified in us when we are satisfied in him. We should follow Jesus because he brings us joy.

The first gospel motive, religious affection, is a joyful motivation for discipleship. But what do we do when we don't feel joyful? Do we resign ourselves to disobedience? Should we abandon following Jesus? Not at all! We fight the *good* fight of faith. It is good to fight for belief in the gospel. We fight for *faith* to believe that obedience to Jesus is better than disobedience. Religious affection is an expression of faith in the gospel, but it does not constitute the whole of faith.[5] Faith also includes trusting God when we *don't* desire him.[6] It is this faith that fights to follow Jesus, even when we don't feel like it. We were recreated in Christ not to run on emotional power but spiritual power—the filling of the Holy Spirit. The power of the Spirit comes to life when we trust in his Word.

Believing God's Warnings and Promises

As Christians we are privileged to possess God's Word, which contains promises and warnings. In Psalm 19:11 David remarks, "Moreover, by them [decrees of God] is your servant *warned*; in keeping them there is great *reward*." God's Word holds out warnings and rewards. Warnings and promises are the second gospel motivation.

We often read over the warnings as if they don't apply. Consider the following warnings written to disciples of Jesus:

- "Now the works of the flesh are evident: sexual immorality, impurity, sensuality, idolatry, sorcery, enmity, strife, jealousy, fits of anger, rivalries, dissensions, divisions, envy, drunkenness, orgies, and things like these. *I warn you, as I warned you before, that those who do such things will not inherit the kingdom of God."* (Gal. 5:19–21)

- "But sexual immorality and all impurity or covetousness must not even be named among you, as is proper among saints. Let there be no filthiness nor foolish talk nor crude joking, which are out of place, but instead let there be thanksgiving. For you may be sure of this, that everyone who is sexually immoral or impure, or who is covetous (that is, an idolater), *has no inheritance in the kingdom of Christ and God."* (Eph. 5:3–5)

These warnings are written to Christians in order to strengthen their faith, promote their joy, and honor the gospel of God. They are not empty threats from a temperamental apostle. They are God-breathed warnings from a loving Lord (2 Tim. 3:16). The sinful patterns and accompanying idols in these lists should not be *characteristic* of Christians. It is one thing to aggressively *fight* our sin, and quite another to passively live with it. These warnings remind us how serious God is about discipleship. He will not be mocked by mile-wide and inch-deep religion. As each text indicates, the proof of our inheritance in the kingdom of God is our present faith. Belief in God's holy warnings can be a gospel motivation if we respond to the warnings by turning to Christ. When I was sleeping with a girlfriend in college, a roommate confronted me with one of God's warnings. Quoting 1 Corinthians 5:11, he told me he didn't want to live with a Christian who lived like an unbeliever: "But now I am writing to you not to associate with anyone who bears the name of brother if he is guilty of sexual immorality or greed, or is an idolater, reviler, drunkard, or swindler—not even to eat with such a one." I don't recall this warning being delivered in a very gracious way, but God used the truth to catalyze repentance! At the time, it was incredibly painful to hear, but God used this warning to prod me toward a new motivation of deeper satisfaction in Christ.

To be a disciple of Jesus is to fight sin with sober belief in God's warnings *and* abounding delight in his promises.[7] Fortunately, God is not a mean-spirited tyrant issuing threats in order to flaunt his power. He is a loving, gracious, just, and infinitely desirable God who binds himself to thousands of promises for the good of his people. Peter tells us that we have been given everything we need for life and godliness through God's very great and precious promises, which make us more like God and less like the world (2 Pet. 1:3–4). Paul reminds us that all the promises of God are "Yes" and "Amen" in Jesus (2 Cor. 1:20). They are doubly trustworthy. Consider the following promises God has made to us, guaranteed in his Son:

- "Delight yourself in the LORD, and he will give you the desires of your heart." (Ps. 37:4)
- "Blessed are the pure in heart, for they shall see God." (Matt. 5.8)
- "And we know that for those who love God all things work together for good, for those who are called according to his purpose." (Rom. 8:28)
- "Beloved, now we are children of God, and it has not appeared as yet what we will be. We know that when He appears, we will be like Him, because we will see Him just as He is." (1 John 3:2 NASB)
- "Humble yourselves under the mighty hand of God, that He may exalt you at the proper time." (1 Pet. 5:6 NASB)

These promises offer us joy, hope, strength, glory, and a place in the kingdom of God. In chapter 7, we will examine some of these, in order to understand how to fight with faith in God's promises when tempted by lust, vanity, and pride. For now, it is important to stress the privilege of trusting God's promises in place of relying on the untrue promises of sin. God motivates our discipleship with both his unblushing promises of reward as well as his sobering warnings of judgment. Daniel Fuller refers to these twin motivations as the pitchfork and the carrot.[8] God prods with his holy warnings and woos us with his staggering promises so that we can live lives of obedience. Both promises and warnings can be gospel motivations. But what should we do when we flat out fail to be motivated by the gospel? When both religious affection and faith in God's promises and warnings fail to motivate us? God offers a third gospel motivation—repentance.

The Gift of Repentance

Repentance is not a one-time act to get us into heaven, but an entire way of life to maintain Christian joy. Repentance isn't a work we tack onto our faith that restores our fellowship with God. Repentance is faith. Tim Chester helpfully illustrates how repentance and faith are one. He writes:

> How do we repent? We repent through faith . . . turning to God in faith and from sin in repentance are the same movement. Try it now. Stand facing the window. Then turn to face the opposite wall. The act of turning from the window and turning towards the wall is one movement. You can't turn towards the wall without turning away from the window. And you can't turn to God in faith without turning away from sin in repentance.[9]

True repentance includes faith.[10] Repentance and faith are two sides of the same gospel coin, one movement made possible by grace. This gospel grace is at our disposal continually in Christ. Martin Luther said: "The entire life of believers is to be one of repentance." Why our entire lives? Because in our everyday failures, we have every opportunity to turn to Jesus for grace and forgiveness. Jesus, himself, exhorted the disciples at

Laodicea to repent: "Those whom I love, I reprove and discipline, so be zealous and repent" (Rev. 3:19).

Unfortunately, repentance is commonly viewed as something we do to get on God's good side. We think to ourselves, "If I feel sorry enough, get angry enough at my sin, then God will forgive me." This view splits the coin of repentance. It assumes that turning from sin is our work, and returning to Christ is God's work. But, remember, repentance is one movement, one coin. To turn from sin is to turn to Christ, a fluid movement of grace, which is a gift from God (Rom. 2:4).

To break repentance down into its two sides, we could say that it is a "turning from" and a "turning to." We turn from our sinful behaviors *and* turn, not to good behaviors, but to Christ. Repentance subsequently overflows in loving obedience. We turn from trust in little gods to trust in the one true God.[11] It is turning from belief in a false promise in order to turn in faith to a true, satisfying promise. Repentance is an exchange of joys, the lesser for the greater. For example, I exchange the joy of self-flattery for the joy of the Lord when I turn away from finding praise in what others say about my preaching, and turn to what God says about me in *his* preaching. God preaches grace to me when he reminds me that I am insufficient in all my preaching, but made sufficient in him as a minister of the gospel: "Not that we are sufficient in ourselves to claim anything as coming from us, but our sufficiency is from God, who has made us sufficient to be ministers of a new covenant" (2 Cor. 3:5–6). When I repent from finding my main joy in what others say about my sermons, and turn to what God says about me in his sermons, I find true joy. I am inadequate as a preacher but more than adequate as a son. You could say this about any role—parent, child, employee. Praise from men is fleeting, but the joy of the Lord is our strength (Neh. 8:10). The same promise applies for those who lack confidence in sharing the gospel with their friends, neighbors, and coworkers. No one is qualified apart from the qualifying work of the Spirit, but all who have the Spirit are qualified. If you have the Spirit, you have more than enough to disciple others. No one is sufficient alone for making disciples. Not a day goes by that we stand self-sufficient before God's righteous gaze. The hope of the gospel, however, is that we are *made sufficient* in Christ. Repentance is a gift from God that compels us to turn away from the fleeting promises of sin and turn to the enduring promises of the gospel.

Repenting Christians are growing Christians. Tim Keller underscores the role of repentance when he says: "All-of-life repentance is the best sign that we are growing deeply and rapidly into the character of Jesus."[12] The purpose of repentance is to lead us into true joy. Repenting is for rejoicing! The intoxicating joy of the Lord exposes our lesser joys for what they are—false and empty—and leads us to faith in the true and rewarding promises of God. A gospel-centered disciple rejects the pursuit of perfection and embraces the gift of repentance. In short, a gospel-centered disciple is a repenting disciple.

Circle of Gospel Motivation

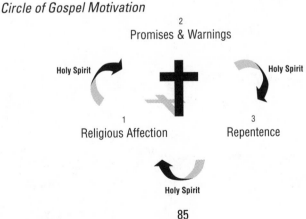

2
Promises & Warnings

Holy Spirit   Holy Spirit

1
Religious Affection

3
Repentence

Holy Spirit

To summarize, gospel motivations are expressed through religious affection, belief in God's warnings and promises, and repentance. To synthesize these three motivations, we can say that 1) religious affection (holy fear and Christ-centered joy) motivates 2) belief in God's warnings and promises which, in turn, 3) motivate a life of repentance when we fail to be motivated by foundational joy in Christ. These three motives come together to form a circle of gospel motivation, surrounding the believer with a host of graces. These motivational graces are applied by the Spirit and move us closer to Jesus. As a result, our joys are altered, the lesser for the greater, and Christ becomes sweeter.[13]

These gospel motivations are compelling, but how can they become dominant in our lives? Where do we get the power to overcome twisted motivations with gospel motivations? In the next chapter, we consider the Spirit as the power for gospel motivation.

5

GOSPEL POWER: THE ESSENTIAL ROLE OF THE HOLY SPIRIT

Perhaps the most neglected motivation for discipleship is the power and presence of the Holy Spirit. This neglect is the result of a variety of factors. One primary factor is theology by reaction. Fear of charismatic excess has driven many evangelicals to emphasize Jesus to the exclusion of the Spirit. This occurs not only in the area of spiritual gifts but also in the practice of discipleship. Those who have taken a cessationist or "open but cautious" position toward spiritual gifts of healing, tongues, and prophecy have carried their caution to an extreme.[1] In turn, "safety barriers" are erected around the third person of the Trinity, effectively dividing him from the second person of the Trinity, Jesus. This reaction to "Spirit-related" excesses has reduced the Spirit to the status of what one member of our church refers to as "the bastard child of the Trinity." Evangelicals rarely emphasize the role of the Spirit in motivation for discipleship. If we are to discover the gospel's power for following Jesus, we will have to teeter over the edge of caution and plunge down the cliff of the Spirit. This chapter may be the most critical of all, as we consider the essential role of the Spirit in discipleship.

No Spirit, No Gospel Holiness

In his vast theological writings, Puritan theologian and pastor, John Owen, frequently refers to a disciple's sanctification as the pursuit of "gospel holiness."[2] What is gospel holiness? In short, gospel holiness is obedience to Christ procured from belief in the gospel, not from one's moral effort. Owen labors to differentiate between gospel holiness and morality. In his distinction, the latter is the product of human effort, not of grace. Although morality and holiness may, at times, look similar on the outside, they are altogether different on the inside. Morality is self-centered; gospel holiness is Christ centered. Morality holds self up high in reaching for moral virtues, but gospel holiness holds Christ up high in virtuous failure and success. Gospel holiness requires the truth of God's Word and his grace to believe and obey the truth. This truth and grace, which comes to us in Jesus (John 1:17), is central to holiness. Owen describes gospel holiness as "peculiarly joined with and limited unto the *doctrine, truth,* and *grace* of the gospel; for holiness is nothing but the implanting, writing, and realizing of the gospel in our souls." Gospel holiness requires both truth and grace. How do we receive grace to believe truth? How is the gospel implanted, written, and realized in us to produce holiness?

Owen takes up gospel holiness in his two volumes on the person and work of the Holy Spirit. He maintains that gospel holiness is impossible *apart from the Holy Spirit.* In fact, his principal reason for writing the first six hundred pages on the Holy Spirit is to show that holiness is "the dispensation and work of the Holy Spirit with respect to the gospel."[3] And again, "There neither is, nor ever was, in the world, nor ever shall be, the least dram of holiness, but what, flowing from Jesus Christ, is communicated by the Spirit, according to the truth and promise of the gospel."[4] To bluntly summarize Owen, it is impossible to have gospel holiness apart from the Holy Spirit. No Spirit, no gospel holiness. You might get morality, even a veneer of Christianity, but no gospel holiness. True joy will escape you. Discipleship devoid of the Spirit's power is no discipleship at all. Apart from the presence and power of the Spirit, our attempt to desire God, believe his promises, fear his warnings, and walk in his ways is absolutely futile. Disciples need more than resolve to believe the gospel; they need the Holy Ghost.

The Presence and Power of the Spirit

How does the Spirit produce gospel holiness? Through his presence and power in disciples of Jesus. The presence of the Spirit is necessary because we are natural born enemies of God (Rom. 5:10), who are spiritually dead in our sin (Eph. 2:5) and darkened in our hearts (Rom. 1:21; Eph. 4:18). It is impossible to express genuine faith in God apart from the Spirit's wooing and life-giving work. The good news, of course, is that by faith in Jesus we can receive new hearts, which are able to trust God. These new, lifeless hearts, however, require the animating presence of the Spirit: *"And I will give you a new heart, and a new spirit I will put within you. And I will remove the heart of stone from your flesh and give you a heart of flesh. And I will put my Spirit within you, and cause you to walk in my statutes and be careful to obey my rules"* (Ezek. 36:26–27). The repeated phrase "put the Spirit," emphasizes the central role of the Holy Spirit in making us new. The newness generated by the Spirit's presence is called *regeneration* (Titus 3:5; Gal. 6:15).

We also need the power of the Spirit. The Spirit not only regenerates but also *motivates* us to obey the Lord. Apart from the presence of Spirit, our new hearts don't beat for God. But when they beat, they generate religious affection and faith in God. Calling upon Ezekiel 36, Paul explains that the regenerating work of the Spirit inevitably motivates good deeds (Titus 3:5–8). These deeds are the natural fruit of newly born sons of God, also called the "fruit of the Spirit" (Galatians 5). This Christlike fruit is the result of our new lives in the Spirit: "If we live by the Spirit, let us also walk by the Spirit" (Gal. 5:25).[5] As soon as we have the Spirit's presence, we have the Spirit's power to live as new creations (Gal. 6:15). The Spirit regenerates us so that our lifeless hearts can beat for God in lives of obedient worship and adoration of the Lord Jesus Christ.

In summary, Scripture shows us a clear connection between the Spirit's regenerating presence and his motivating power. Disciples possess gospel holiness through the power and presence of the Spirit. How does this work practically? What does reliance on the Spirit look like? I suggest we learn how to rely on the Holy Spirit in two main ways: first, by observing how *Jesus* relied on the Spirit, and second, by cultivating a similar *relationship* with the Spirit.

The Presence of the Spirit in the Person of Jesus

Although Jesus had no need for regeneration, he depended on the presence of the Spirit to motivate his obedience to the Father. Luke, theologian of the Holy Spirit, goes out of his way to emphasize the necessity of the presence and power of the Spirit in the life and ministry of Jesus. In accordance with Scriptures, Jesus was anointed with the Holy Spirit prior to his public ministry (Isa. 61:1; Luke 4:18). This anointing lines Jesus up with the prophets who possessed the Spirit in a unique way. In Luke 3, Jesus is baptized by the Holy Spirit and approved by the Father for ministry (21–22), but proceeds into the wilderness, compelled by the Spirit, for a forty-day trial. He emerges from the wilderness "in the power of the Spirit," succeeding where Adam and Israel failed in their "temptations" (Luke 4:14). Next, Jesus makes his way to Nazareth to announce he is the much awaited, Spirit-anointed Messiah the Jews have been longing for (Luke 4:18–21). After being anointed with the Spirit, Jesus's ministry is marked by a cycle of prophetic teachings on the kingdom of God, performances of exorcism, and profound healings. How did he accomplish this? It was the motivating power of the Spirit that enabled Jesus to endure temptation and live in obedience to the Father.

If Jesus required the Spirit for life and faith, how much more do we need the Spirit? Will Walker helpfully illustrates this point by posing the question: "If you had the choice between Jesus and the Holy Spirit for your 'discipler,' who would you choose?"[6] Most of us would gravitate toward Jesus; after all, he is the Master discipler. However, disciples need the Spirit's power to truly follow Jesus (John 20:21–22; Acts 1:8). We should choose the Holy Spirit. When we consider Jesus, very often we look to him as an example of godly character but fail to see his example of dependence upon the Spirit. The life of Jesus is exemplary not just in what he did but also how he did it. Jesus was not immune to temptation or impervious to suffering. He fought the good fight of faith but he did not fight it alone. Jesus did not sever himself from the Trinity in order to accomplish his mission. He remained in communion with the Father and dependent upon the Spirit. The Spirit empowered and motivated everything Jesus did. In order to discern how the Spirit motivates following Jesus, we will examine how he empowered Jesus in two areas: decision making and temptation.

Decision Making

After his baptism, Jesus was "led by the Spirit in the wilderness for forty days, being tempted by the devil" (Luke 4:1–2). Notice that the Spirit played a directive role in the life of the Son of God. Mark tells us that the Spirit "drove" Jesus into the wilderness (Mark 1:12). Jesus clearly relied on the Spirit for direction. This sensitivity to the directing influence of the Holy Spirit is characteristic of the disciples in the book of Acts. Philip is directed to speak to the Ethiopian eunuch (Acts 8). Peter is directed to the house of Cornelius (Acts 10). The Jerusalem Council is directed in their decision making (Acts 15). Paul is directed to not go to Bithynia (Acts 16). How is the Spirit directing your life? Very often, our modern, self-reliant sensibilities cut the Spirit right out of everyday decision making. Rarely do we request or expect the Spirit's direction. Yet, we are repeatedly told to "walk" in the Spirit throughout the Bible (Ezek. 36:27; Rom. 8:4; Gal. 5:16, 25) and to make decisions by seeking the Lord (Prov. 5:4–6; James 4:13–15). Being motivated by the Spirit should affect not just moral decisions but also our general approach to life. Paul tells us to "be filled with the Spirit" (Eph. 5:18). How often do we start our day by requesting a fresh filling of the Spirit's power for the day that lies ahead? Instead, we assume his presence and barrel forward. Our assumption of the Spirit reveals a self-reliant faith. Instead of starting and continuing our days in our own strength, what would it look like to fight for faith with utter dependence upon the power and direction of the Holy Spirit?

The disciples in the New Testament often followed their Lord expecting unplanned change. We, on the other hand, like to manage our lives in order to eliminate unplanned change. We regulate everything through clocks, calendars, PDAs, smartphones, routines, and rhythms. When our planned course of action is disrupted, we frequently respond impatiently or angrily. What if you began to expect unplanned change and interpreted it as an opportunity to rely on the Spirit? Obstacles, challenges, and trials would take on a very different meaning. Instead of becoming inconveniences and injustices, unplanned change could become an opportunity to rely on the Spirit to discern God's will and purpose in our circumstances. The person cutting us off on the highway might become a reminder to fight sinful busyness or celebrate God's protection. When heading to a coffee shop, we might ask the Spirit to take us wherever God wants us be and to whomever he might want us to see. One very practical way we can be motivated by the Spirit in our discipleship is to expect unplanned change and respond to the Spirit in those circumstances. For example:

- Instead of getting angry or frustrated when unplanned things occur, ask the Spirit to show you his purposes in the circumstances.
- Instead of just deciding which restaurant or coffee shop you want to go to, ask the Spirit to lead you.
- Instead of jamming your calendar full of personal preferences, pray and ask the Spirit to guide you as you plan your week, month, or year.

Now that we have considered the Spirit's role in decision making, we will examine how Jesus relied on him in the face of temptation.

Overcoming Temptation

The necessity of the Spirit to obey Jesus as Lord is replete in Paul's letters (especially 1 Corinthians, Ephesians, Philippians, Galatians). When confronted with temptation, Paul underscores that victory comes through the Spirit: "But I say, walk by the Spirit, and you will not gratify the desires of the flesh" (Gal. 5:16). Our flesh longs for a variety of things, including control and sinful self-reliance. How do we combat these fleshly patterns? Paul tells us explicitly that the way we avoid the desires of the flesh is to "walk by the Spirit." How then do we walk by the Spirit? Many of us have become so dependent upon ourselves that we don't have a clue of how to walk by the Spirit. Like stumbling infants, walking in the Spirit looks like we are learning to walk for the very first time.

The Spirit will direct us into undesirable circumstances. He led Jesus to fast for forty days, in a human body, in the wilderness, under the attack of the Devil. The leading of the Spirit sometimes includes suffering, but even that suffering is designed for our gospel holiness. Consider how Jesus relied on the Spirit during his wilderness temptations. During each temptation, Jesus relived the temptations of Israel during their forty years in the wilderness. Yet, instead of failing at each temptation of food, faith, and fame, Jesus succeeded. How? He relied on the power of the Spirit to believe the promises of God. When faced with the promises of Satan, Jesus responded by faith in God's promises. He realized God's words were true and reliable and that the Devil's words were false and unreliable. Jesus trusted in the promises of God by the power of the Spirit. Let's examine Jesus's temptations more closely.

When tempted by food, Jesus refused the temptation to turn stones into bread during his fast. Instead, he kept his Spirit-led course by reciting and trusting Deuteronomy 8:3: "Man does not live by bread alone, but man lives by every word that comes from the mouth of the LORD." By the power of the Spirit, Jesus refused to distract himself from fasting and devotion to the

Father, and instead chose to trust in God's unfailing, soul-nourishing promises and truths. In this, Jesus is exemplary for those who are overstuffed with false promises and undernourished with true promises. In his weakened estate, how could Jesus resist such a temptation—fresh bread in a dry wilderness? He walked closely with the Spirit into undesirable circumstances—a forty-day fast in the wilderness—where he suffered well. Taking up the failures of Israel and all humanity, Jesus overcame temptation through his relationship with the Holy Spirit.

In his second temptation, Jesus was tempted to fame by flippantly throwing himself off the temple to be caught by angels. In response, he recited and trusted in Deuteronomy 6:16: "You shall not put the LORD God to the test." By the power of the Spirit, Jesus believed it was better to trust and revere God than to one-up the Devil through a miraculous display. By resting in God's humbling design of the wilderness, Jesus shows us the importance of faithfully relying on the Spirit's direction and power.

In the third and final temptation, Jesus was promised worldly power and glory in exchange for worshiping the Devil. Jesus spots the false promises, reciting and trusting in Deuteronomy 6:13: "It is the LORD your God you shall fear. Him you shall serve." By the power of the Spirit, in the lowliest of places, Jesus refused the temptation to ascend to the heights of power and believed that it was better to worship the one true God. In each temptation of food, faith, and fame, Jesus succeeds where Israel and all humanity fail. How did he do it? Through Spirit-empowered faith in the promises of God. Jesus followed the leading of the Spirit, relied on his power, and trusted in the promises of God. The Spirit enabled him to trust in what was true in the face of what was false. Jesus is exemplary, not merely in his holiness but also in his reliance on the Holy Spirit.

Communion with the Holy Spirit

Without the Spirit, we are powerless to believe the gospel of Jesus, but those who are in Christ have *the most powerful motivation* for discipleship present in them—the very Spirit of God! The challenge, then, is to actually know the Spirit so that he becomes our motivation in following Jesus. What we need is a *relationship* with the Holy Spirit.

In chapter 1, I mentioned my first encounter with discipleship, at age twenty. Six years later, I began a relationship with the Holy Spirit. For two decades I simply assumed his presence. Like a neglected sibling, the Spirit remained faithfully present but relatively unknown. He was, as Francis Chan has put it, my "forgotten God."[7] Two men were influential in reacquainting me with my forgotten God. The first was Richard Lovelace, author of *Dynamics of Spiritual Life.*[8] I had the privilege of taking two courses from Dr. Lovelace while I was in seminary. It was during the dynamics class that I was deeply challenged to know the Spirit. Lovelace shared with us how he made a point of communing with each person of the Trinity throughout the day by praying to the Father in the morning, the Son in the evening, and the Spirit in the afternoon. I began this practice immediately and continue it to this day. Lovelace struggles from a stroke that caused the left side of his face to droop and he has limited physical ability. Despite this, you can tell that Lovelace has been with Jesus and is acquainted with the Spirit. His book *Dynamics of Spiritual Life,* is as much a reflection of his life as it is the history and elements of spiritual renewal. I recall riding with him to eat pizza one day. On the way there, he exuded a general happiness in the Lord, an awareness of the Spirit to such a degree that he missed the turn! His kind demeanor and genuine affection for God were abundantly clear as we ate. More could be said about

Lovelace's theology of the Spirit, but I will leave you with his books for that.[9]

The second person instrumental in reacquainting me with the Spirit was Colin Gunton. I've never met Gunton, but I am deeply grateful for his writings and sermons. About a year after meeting Lovelace, I read Gunton's book *The Triune Creator*.[10] While reading the book in the quiet guest bedroom of our garage apartment, I collapsed to my knees in tears, repentant over my neglect of the Spirit. I choked out prayers of repentance for failing to adore, know, and rely upon the Holy Spirit. I was met with a sweet forgiveness and spiritual sensation that attuned me to the third person of the Trinity. I have continued to commune with the Spirit ever since. To some this may seem elementary, and to others, intimidating. Regardless of your experience, the Spirit is eager to commune with us and to empower us for gospel holiness.

Communion is a word that has fallen out of practice. What does it mean to "commune"? To commune with someone is to share something with him or her that is of mutual benefit. We commune with a friend over a great piece of music, a film, or a theological truth when we both exult in its creativity, excellence, or brilliance. John Owen defines communion as "the sharing of good things between persons who are mutually delighted being cemented together by some union."[11] Communion, then, is not just shared delight, but the "cementing effect" of that shared delight between two persons.

You have probably experienced communion with close friends. What makes a friend close? You are close, not because of proximity, but because you share a delight in some of the same things (music, film, food, values, beliefs), and that shared delight has a cementing effect, which creates a close bond between friends. Prayer fosters this bond with God, cementing our souls with him through shared delight in the gospel of grace. All too often we eliminate the Holy Spirit from our communion with God. We live as functional bi-nitarians, communing with the Father and the Son, not Trinitarians— communing with Father, Son, and Spirit. In order to experience the Spirit's power, we need know the Spirit as a Person, to begin a relationship with him through prayer. Here are a few ways to begin:

- You may need to begin with repentance over your neglect of the Spirit. Confess your sinful self-reliance to the Father and the Spirit, asking the Son for forgiveness, and thanking God for the gift of the Spirit.
- Make a point of addressing the Spirit throughout the day in ways that reflect his role in your life (understanding, discernment, decision making, power to overcome sin, desire for God, faith in the gospel, etc.)
- Memorize and meditate on texts that show you who the Spirit is so that you can get to know him (Ex. 31:3; Num. 27:18; 1 Sam. 16:13; Joel 2:28–29; Acts; Romans 8, 15; 1 Corinthians 2; 2 Corinthians 3; Galatians 3–6).
- Rejoice in the gift of the Spirit as a Person who indwells us with power to believe the gospel, glorify, and enjoy God!

Communion with the Spirit brings us a general happiness and contentment that cannot be found anywhere else. Communing with the Holy Spirit produces a vertical relationship with the Lord that has horizontal results. When we repersonalize the Spirit, he reintegrates us as disciples who have a whole way of living wholly under God's redemptive reign in Christ. The more we relate to the Spirit, the less we will be concerned about balancing vertical and horizontal discipleship. Spirit-empowered belief in Jesus Christ as Lord leads to an integration of piety and mission. This communion with God takes us deeper into holiness *and* sends us further into mission. As we relate to the Spirit, he empowers us to believe the gospel of Jesus Christ. How do we tap into this power? How does communion with the Spirit produce gospel holiness?

Surrendering to the Spirit

I'm discovering that most of the time the power of the Spirit is subtle, not showy. The Spirit is present in our subtle inclinations to serve our spouses, do what's right, read the Bible, love the marginalized, make disciples, and commune with God. He is that renewing presence that says: "Choose what is good, right, and true." He is that tug toward self-sacrifice for the good of others. He is that challenge to boldly tell someone how Jesus is changing your life. He is the Person that brings Scripture to mind and coaxes you to believe it. He is the one who prompts you to pray for others. He is the one who restrains you from clicking on that image on the Internet, making that purchase, or silently judging someone. He prompts you to encourage a friend, to praise the good in a coworker, or to rejoice in God's remarkable grace. If you are in Christ, you have the Spirit, and he prompts you all the time. We simply need to surrender to his prompting!

If all we need to experience the Spirit's power is to surrender to his prompting, then why is communion with the Spirit so important? I can think of two important reasons. First, those who are in communion with the Spirit are more likely to sense his promptings. Have you ever noticed how out of step you can be with a friend or spouse when you haven't spent much time together, how mechanical the conversation can be? When we are out of communion with the Spirit, it is very difficult to discern his promptings. Second, as Westerners we easily mistake the presence of the Spirit for our own conscience or "enlightened" reason. When we make this mistake, we easily dismiss the promptings of the Spirit as mere rational options. For instance, the Spirit may prompt me to do the dishes, but I don't have to do them because I did them yesterday. Decision making is reduced to a inner dialogue with our reason, not an opportunity to relate the person of the Spirit. We succumb to a ploy of the Deceiver who would have us "mistake" the Spirit for fleeting personal preference or a rational option. When we do this, we depersonalize the Spirit.

When we depersonalize the Spirit, it becomes much easier to disobey or deny the Lord. When we reduce the promptings of Spirit to options, we miss out on communion with God. We deny his power and fellowship. Don't be deceived. The Spirit is prompting you all the time to believe the gospel, to serve others, to choose what is good and true, and to walk in gospel holiness. Satan wants to thwart your communion with God. He doesn't want you to enter into a conversation with the Spirit. He wants us to converse with "our reason," dismissing the subtle presence of the Spirit and his power to motivate holiness. How many times have we rationalized away an opportunity to communicate the gospel? "They are in a hurry." "She would think I'm weird." "I don't even know that person." These rational objections didn't stop Philip with the Ethiopian, or Peter with his kinfolk, or Paul with strangers. Instead of assuming a dialogue with your reason, enter into dialogue with the Spirit. Talk to him and ask him for clarity, direction, and power to believe the gospel. In a word, surrender! Surrender to the Spirit's promptings, follow his nudging, and talk to him about it along the way. When we surrender to the Spirit we become ourselves in Jesus. We walk in a shared delight that so cements us to the Lord that we develop a missional holiness. Communion with the Spirit releases the power of the Spirit so that we can follow Jesus and make disciples.

Returning to the Trinity

When we refuse to rely on the gospel of grace, we trivialize the Trinity by not trusting the Father's promises, selling out the Son's sacrifice, and slighting the Spirit's power. We cheapen the atoning work of Jesus by trying to add or subtract from the cross. We dismiss the Spirit as a forgettable God, relying on our own effort or reason in decision making and temptation. As we have seen, self-reliant legalism and spiritual license produce very unattractive disciples who fail to behold and become the image of Jesus. In order to avoid twisted motivations for discipleship, I have sketched three major gospel motivations—religious affections, promises and warnings, and repentance and faith. However, all three of these motivations are powerless apart from the Holy Spirit. The Spirit is the motivation behind the motivation, the personal presence of God's power inclining us to believe the gospel. As it turns out, the gospel is not enough. We desperately need the Spirit to have affection for Christ, to believe his promises, to heed his warnings, to repent from our sin, and to trust Jesus. Without the Spirit, we cannot believe the gospel. When we neglect God's Spirit within us, we will fail to experience the joy of gospel holiness. Without the motivating cause of the Spirit, our efforts to believe the gospel are in vain. In the words of Owen, "The immediate efficient *cause* of all gospel holiness is the Spirit of God."[12] We need the Spirit, his presence and his power, to believe the gospel of Jesus Christ. Spirit-empowered faith in the gospel is required not only to become disciples but also to continue as disciples. No Spirit, no gospel holiness.

The wonderful news is that all disciples of Jesus are indwelt with the Spirit. He is working with us, not against us, for gospel holiness. Gospel holiness can be as simple as surrendering to the promptings of the Spirit and as difficult as fighting the flesh. He wants to commune with us in everyday decision making. God has called us to surrender to his Spirit and to fight our flesh. We have every power necessary in the Spirit to fight for the noble image and beauty of Jesus. Father, Son, and Spirit are collaborating for our gospel-centered discipleship. Along with the power of the Spirit, God has given us another grace—the church. Disciples of Jesus are part of a *community* that fights the fight of faith. The Spirit indwells and empowers us to be gospel-centered communities that fight for communion with God in everyday life.

PART THREE

Applying the Gospel

6

COMMUNAL DISCIPLESHIP: THE THREE CONVERSIONS

So far we have addressed the definition of a disciple (part 1) and the motivation of a disciple (part 2). In part 3, we turn to the practice of a disciple. How can disciples apply the gospel in practice? This chapter will argue that the gospel converts disciples three times, not just once—converting us to Christ, to church, and to mission. We begin by examining the formative role of community, followed by purpose of mission, in the lives of gospel-centered disciples. We will show from Scripture that community and mission are second and third conversions that follow our conversion to Jesus. Without all three conversions, a disciple is incomplete.

Rediscovering the Gospel in Community

For years Haydn coasted in his faith. Burned out by the legalistic culture of his Christian college experience, his postgrad years were a combination of disillusionment and disengagement with church. Church attendance was infrequent. Instead of investing in spiritual things, he decided to pursue his career, start a family, and carve out a spot in the good life. He climbed the career ladder pretty quickly. Before he knew it, he was a father of two, living in a half-a-million-dollar home in SoCo, and enjoying a new community among fellow cyclists. What could be better? But after a while, his good life seemed flat. He tried a few things to jump-start it, including increased church attendance, but nothing seemed to work.

One day Nate, a former-musician friend now obsessed with the gospel, shared with Haydn how God was changing his life *through community*. Nate would eventually become a pastor in our church. Skeptical but interested, Haydn began to ask more questions and even invited me over to his daughter's birthday party. The more Haydn learned, the more he was intrigued. Something was different about this church. They cared about one another and for their city. Haydn joined the church in social service projects and even showed up at some house church gatherings. Deep down, he knew this was what he had been longing for, something much better than the so-called good life. Eventually, he began asking God if he should sell his house and become a missionary. He kept his house and became a missionary—to his own people—in Austin, Texas. Haydn was converted to Christ and the church in a new way. He was beginning to understand the gospel in a way he never had.

It wasn't until Haydn started sharing his struggles with others that he really sensed significant change. As he and his family integrated into the church, Haydn joined a fight club (I address fight clubs more in chapters 7 and 8). He began meeting with two other disciples who were serious about fighting sin, enjoying God, living in community, and serving the city. It was through these relationships, through being the church, that Haydn rediscovered the power of the gospel. He came to understand that the gospel of grace wasn't just something that makes you a disciple; it matures you as a disciple. He understood that the gospel frees imperfect people to cling to a perfect Christ, which changes everything. He began to grow in his understanding of theology, community, and mission. Haydn and his wife, Tiffany, hosted member classes, city groups, and eventually became deacons in the church. What changed Haydn's view of faith and church? A *community* of gospel-centered disciples.[1] He encountered a group of people that made grace, not rules, central to their following Jesus. Instead of emphasizing religious performance, they focused on the grace of God. Several years later, his fight club continues to meet regularly to pray, share life, and fight sin *together*. Through these relationships, Haydn has rediscovered the power of the gospel and the preciousness of Christ. Commenting on his experience he wrote: "The gospel is more than a one-time event that 'saved' me. I have learned, and continue to learn, that the gospel is something I need every minute of everyday. It changes me as a husband, a father, a friend, an employee, a manager. . . . Everything, everyday. This was a 'light bulb' moment. Furthermore, I have seen the gospel in this community. As imperfect as it is, it is true to the gospel."[2]

The One-Third Gospel

Unfortunately, Haydn's story is the exception and not the rule. The American landscape is dotted with churchless Christianity. Church has been reduced to a weekly or biweekly event. Instead of *being the church*, we have fallen into merely *doing church*, and far too often our doing is disconnected from being. We have devolved from being Jesus-centered communities into loose collections of spiritually minded individuals.

Churches today have more in common with shopping malls, fortresses, and cemeteries than they do the church of the New Testament. They have become consumerist, doctrinaire, lifeless institutions, not Jesus-centered missional communities. Why this gross distortion? There are far too many reasons to discuss here, but a fundamental reason Christianity in America is both churchless and in decline is due to the fact it is characterized by a one-third gospel.[3] This one-third gospel is hardly the gospel at all. It focuses on Jesus's death and resurrection as a doctrine to be believed, not on Jesus as a Person to be trusted and obeyed. The gospel has been reduced to a personal ticket to heaven. But the biblical gospel is much more than personal conversion to gain a reservation in heaven. It is conversion to Jesus Christ as Lord. Moreover, the gospel has two more "thirds." The gospel calls us into *community* and onto *mission.*[4]

The Three Conversions

When we are converted, we are not converted to Christ alone. It was Martin Luther who first spoke of three conversions: conversion of the heart, conversion of the mind, and conversion of the purse. He focused on what needs *to be converted in man.* It is also important to consider *what man is converted to.* The gospel converts our hearts, minds, and money, but it also converts us to something. When we are converted, we are converted to Christ, to church, and to mission. New Testament authors repeatedly use metaphors for the church that reveal a need for three conversions. Each of the three conversions is present in the three primary church metaphors of harvest, body, and temple. These theological metaphors show us that the three conversions of the gospel are not three options, but three essentials that constitute biblical discipleship. Each conversion reflects an aspect of what it means to be a disciple. The relational aspect is present in conversion to community, and the missional aspect is present in conversion to mission. Let's consider how the gospel converts us to Christ, to church, and to mission.

The Body

When we are converted to *Jesus*, we are converted *into his church*. Jesus did not die on a bloody cross to gather a loose collection of souls bound for heaven, but to create a new community as the proof of his gospel to the world. The church is naturally a community of gospel-centered disciples. The problem, however, is that we have a very unnatural, distorted view of the gospel. When we think of the gospel, we think primarily of individual conversion. On the contrary, the Bible typically presents conversion as a communal phenomenon.

Consider the biblical metaphor of the human body. When we receive Jesus Christ as Lord and Head (Col. 2:6), we are immediately knit into his body (Col. 1:18; 2:2). The body is knit together with the ligaments and sinews of love and truth producing a unified, whole body (Ephesians 4; Colossians 3). Those who have been converted to Jesus are converted to his body. They speak the truth in love to one another (Eph. 4:15, 25), forgive and forbear with one another (Col. 3:13), and teach and admonish one another in wisdom (Col. 3:16). To reject our conversion to the church is to disobey the Head and distort his body. We are not converted to a disembodied Head; we are converted to an embodied Christ, which includes Head and body. Unfortunately, many of us have a disembodied Jesus, perhaps a bobble-head Jesus, all Head and very little body. When we practice discipleship that focuses on Jesus as a disembodied Head, we distort his body, and we distort his gospel. Jesus didn't die and rise to rapture individual disciples, but to make a community that reflects his glory through dependence on one another. When we join Jesus, we join his family and his mission. As we will see, when Jesus Christ is Lord, he integrates disciples into a missional church family.

Interestingly, when the church embraces the second conversion to community, very often the third conversion to mission follows. A Jesus-centered community is an attractive community—a community that encourages, forgives, serves, loves, and invites non-Christians into its community. The gospel reconciles people to God and to one another, creating a single new community comprised of an array of cultures and languages to make one new humanity (Col. 2:15). This new humanity reconciles its differences (Col. 2:14–16) in the commonality of the gospel. It is both local and global. As the body grows, a redeemed, multiethnic, intergenerational, economically and culturally diverse humanity emerges. When we act as the church toward one another, we display the gracious, redemptive reign of Jesus to the world. As Jesus's redemptive reign breaks into this world, the church grows into the full stature of Christ.

In the New Testament, the word for "stature" is used to refer to both physical (Luke 2:52; 19:3) and spiritual growth (Eph. 4:13). In Ephesians and Colossians, Paul uses this imagery to refer to the historic and progressive work of the gospel in reconciling people to God and to one another. In other words, the full stature of Christ is the result of the gospel's work inwardly among its members and outwardly in the harvest (Ephesians 2, 4; Colossians 2). It is the result of disciples who make disciples. Growing into the full stature of Christ is a missional growth.[5] The body metaphor shows us that disciples of Christ are converted three times—to the Head, the body, and the full stature of Christ—to Christ, church, and mission. The family grows inwardly and outwardly into the full stature of Christ (Eph. 4:13–14). Our growth into the full stature of Christ is a missional growth.

Lord of the Harvest

The second church metaphor is the field or harvest. Jesus is Lord of the harvest (Luke 10) and we are his field (1 Corinthians 3). As a field, the church grows through planting, sowing, fertilizing, weed pulling, and watering in community. We need encouragement, correction, rebuke, empathy, prayer, truth telling, and promise reminding. Although God ultimately causes our growth, God has chosen the community to facilitate that growth! Jesus is Lord not merely of individual wheat stalks but also of the self-nurturing field. We grow *together*. If we do not share life together, we stunt the growth of the church. In order to nurture the field and increase the harvest, we must be involved in one another's lives. This means surrendering our "rights" to individualistic privacy, convenience, and comfort.

Steady State Community

In Austin City Life, we practice conversion-to-community through our city groups. City groups are where we are the church to one another and to the city. When I started the first city group, someone asked: "Do we have to meet every week? Can we meet every other week?" To which I replied, "How can we be family if we only gather once every two weeks?" This, of course, threatens our convenience. Two and a half hours a week, over a meal, giving and receiving grace from people who are very different from us, isn't natural. We are used to being accountable only to ourselves. If we are honest, our highest obligation of love is to self—doing, saying, and feeling whatever we like. Interestingly, self-love is the paradigm for true love. Jesus tells us to "love [our] neighbor as [ourselves]" (Lev. 19:18; Matt. 19:19). Disciples should do, say, and try to feel what is best for others, not for themselves. In doing so, they find deeper contentment as

111

they live out their disciples-in-community purpose. To be blunt, disciples of Jesus should regularly sacrifice privacy, convenience, and comfort in order to love and serve others.

Our city groups have become much more than a weekly meeting. Many of them live in what we refer to as "steady state community." True community is a steady state of social, gospel, and missional connections, which results in connecting over meals, in social settings, and on mission. It isn't unusual for our city groups to gather multiple times a week (often in pockets), at a baseball game, bar, in the projects, neighborhood, or at a restaurant. For many, this starts as a discipline to love and serve others, but slowly matures into deeper community and love. The challenge of loving others as we love ourselves confronts our deep-down idolatries. It exposes our functional worship of individual privacy, convenience, and comfort. However, when we practice this kind of community, it becomes a remarkable display of the gospel to the world.

The conversion to mission in this church metaphor is expressed through the harvest. The church is a field of future laborers (Luke 10:2) who go out to increase the harvest. As we go, we pray to the Lord of the harvest to increase the harvest through our mission. One of the ways the harvest grows is by inviting not-yet disciples into steady-state community.[6] The overlap of Christians and non-Christians can happen naturally over meals, at birthday parties, and in service to your city. It is here that people get to witness communal discipleship, and it is here that disciples can witness in community.

When you gather like this, be sure to look for opportunities to talk about the deeper things of life, to love people well by listening to their struggles, doubts, and fears. Share how the gospel has helped you in your own struggles, doubts, and fears.

Apply the gospel to yourself out loud with non-Christians. Be transparent and authentic with them. Instead of hiding your faith and the deep grace you have found in Jesus, talk about it in natural ways. As you do, be sure to pray to the Lord of the harvest for spiritual fruit, and then watch the harvest grow! In summary, the harvest metaphor reveals the three conversions as conversion to the Lord, to the field, and to the harvest—Christ, church, and mission.

The Temple

The final church metaphor is the temple or building. In 1 Peter 2, Jesus is described as the Cornerstone of the temple or building of God (Ps. 118:22). A cornerstone is the most important stone in the whole building. The entire building depends on it for structural integrity. However, the cornerstone alone does not constitute the entire building. As Peter points out, the temple is comprised of other "living stones" that together comprise a "chosen race, a royal priesthood, a holy nation, a people for his own possession" (1 Pet. 2:9). The Cornerstone, together with the rest of the stones, form a majestic temple in which the glory of the Lord dwells. We are the stones, held together in Christ, made alive in the gospel to minister as priests to one another. Jesus redeemed us to comprise his holy temple. As we minister to one another, we should promote one another's holiness. Kristin shares an example of how she has been converted to the church as a "living stone" that ministers the gospel of grace to others.

> It came to my attention that one of my friends was bitter and angry with those around her. She was ready to leave the church. I knew I needed to sit and have a talk with her. However, there was a large part of me that didn't want to confront

her. I was afraid of what she would think of me, of what she might say about me. I was worried about myself, and held off from loving her well, because I was afraid of what she would think of me. I lacked faith that the Holy Spirit could and would be at work in both of us.

After praying and reading about the issue, I realized that I did not need to go over a laundry list of her offenses. What she needed was a sister, who would lovingly look with her at what the gospel has to say about anger, and create space for her to confess, repent, and pray for forgiveness. It was a time for me to be someone who actually loved her, pointing her back to Jesus who loves her better than anyone could. After we met, she felt blessed by the time and asked for forgiveness from those she had hurt.

Perhaps the greatest change of all happened in me! At first, I thought it was my responsibility to confront her as a ministry leader. But then I began to ask myself: "Would I do this with others if I didn't feel the pressure of my position description? Isn't this a part of my role as a disciple of Christ?" I fear man when I forget Jesus. The gospel is powerful, and having fresh encounters with Jesus in the gospel allows me to walk in the courage of the Holy Spirit. While I may not have it all together, God can use me just as he uses those around me, to speak into my life.[7]

Kristin reminds us of the loving obligation we have to speak truth and grace into others' lives. Her story also reminds us that God's grace agenda works best in community, where both those who correct and those who are corrected can change. Notice what she learned about herself: "I fear man when I forget Jesus." Conversely, when she stepped out in faith, remembering Jesus, she loved man. As a result, both of them reflected the image of Christ more. God wants to use us to minister his grace to one another. He has given us his Spirit to build his church into an increasing temple of glory, which shows off our chief Cornerstone.

Switching metaphors, Peter turns stones into sojourners in order to emphasize our corporate responsibility to "abstain from the passions of the flesh" and to love one another: "Honor everyone. Love the brotherhood. Fear God. Honor the emperor" (1 Pet. 2:17). Living stones prove their vitality by being cemented to one another in Christ and ministering to one another in love. This requires intentionality, hard conversations, transparency, and prayer, as we saw in Kristin's story. Increasing the glory in his temple comes about when priests take seriously their responsibility to "love the brotherhood." Jesus's glory and our good are on the line. Our conversion to community is clear: conversion to the Cornerstone is conversion to living stones. How this metaphor conveys our conversion to mission is, perhaps, less obvious.

As living stones in a holy temple, we have been called to display the holiness of God and proclaim the excellencies of Christ (1 Pet. 2:9). Our holiness should compel people outside the church, attracting them to Christ. As living stones, our lives should spill over in a vibrant witness to the Jesus who has changed us. I was recently getting my hair cut by a new hairdresser. As we talked, she inquired about our church. I shared our commitment to renewing the city socially, spiritually, and culturally with the gospel of Jesus. She was intrigued. I gave her examples of our city-renewing activity. As the haircut ended, I shared why we do all this. I said to her: "The reason we do all this isn't because we are great; it's because God is great. I'm not even a great pastor. The reason I do all this, Amber, is because I'm quite taken with Jesus. I've had a profound, personal encounter with him." Living stones speak about their life in Christ. They can't help it. Amber hasn't become a living stone yet. We're still talking about the gospel, but when anyone becomes a disciple of Christ, the temple expands and a living stone is added. God's grand plan, from the beginning, was for the garden-temple of Eden to expand throughout the whole world, to be populated with new stones who worship Jesus Christ, the great Cornerstone.[8] The gospel converts us three times—to the Cornerstone, the living stones, and the expansion of the temple—to Christ, church, and mission.

When we believe the gospel, we are converted three times. This understanding of the gospel has massive implications. Failure to convert to the church and to mission is a failure to grasp the gospel. When we are not gospel centered, we will veer off into comfortable individualism and abandon the mission. However, if our primary conversion is to Jesus Christ as Lord (Col. 2:6), we will grow in loving others as ourselves and grow into the full stature of Christ. Complete disciples yield missional holiness.

The lordship of Jesus is present in the church metaphors as Lord of the harvest, Head of the body, and Cornerstone of the temple. It is important to note that Jesus is Lord, not church or mission. Be careful you don't get that mixed up. Both church and mission will fail you, and you will fail in your church and mission. The good news is that Jesus never fails. Dietrich Bonhoeffer helpfully points out that every Christian must have their ideal community shattered before entering into true community. He writes: "He who loves his dream of a community more than the Christian community itself becomes a destroyer of the latter."[9] The same can be said of mission. He who loves his dream of mission more than he loves Jesus will become a destroyer of mission. Community and mission are second to Jesus's glory, but Jesus pursues his glory through community and mission.

To make church or mission our primary conversion is an act of idolatry. Jesus alone is Lord; however, the lordship of Jesus does not stand alone. As Lord of all, Jesus calls us into a whole way of following him in the whole of life, including our relationships with the church and our call into his mission.

Whether these concepts are new to you or not, they probably sound challenging. The three conversions fly in the face of individualistic, consumeristic values of Western society. Repenting from Western values and returning to gospel values takes a church, which is why God gave us one another. As the church, we can live, grow, and encourage one another to believe in a gospel that reflects all three conversions. Instead of reducing the gospel to a distorted third, we can join together in living out a whole gospel in the whole of life, conversion to Christ, church, and mission. We get to struggle with and for one another to believe that Jesus is better, richer, sweeter, and deeper than anything else in this world. As we do, we share our struggles and our Savior with others. That is what disciples do. They fight the good fight of faith with one another and for others. In the next chapter, we will explore how to do this practically through fight clubs, small fighting communities that encourage one another to beat up sin and believe the gospel of Christ.

7

PRACTICAL DISCIPLESHIP: PUTTING THE GOSPEL INTO PRACTICE

The growing popularity of ultimate fighting and the emergence of real fight clubs are telling. In basements across the country, white urban professionals meet to fight one another with fists, chairs, sticks, and even computer keyboards. One Silicon Valley fight club uses domestic items as weapons such as: dust busters, toilet seats, cookie sheets, and rods wrapped with Martha Stewart magazines. When asked why they fight, they explain that "when you punch somebody or when you get punched there is a kind of grounding effect that makes you really feel alive." The pain awakens them from the numbness of their mundane lives. In these fight clubs men fight to feel alive, to be reminded of their own mortality in an increasingly digitized world.

These fight clubs were inspired by Chuck Palahniuk's book by the same name, which was popularized by the film *Fight Club*, starring Brad Pitt and Edward Norton. Although I can't recommend the film due to some of its content, Palahniuk's *Fight Club* does depict the struggle to recover identity in a postmodern, media-saturated world. It shows us that the world is charged with bogus images of what it means to be truly human. In underground fight clubs, groups of men meet after hours in basements and back alleys to fight one another barefoot, bare chested, and bare fisted. It's a bloody ordeal. In a speech just prior to a fight club, Tyler Durden charges the men: "We are the middle children of history, man. No purpose or place. We have no great war, or great depression. Our great war is a spiritual war. Our great depression is our lives. We've all been raised by television to believe that one day we'll all be millionaires and movie gods and rock stars—but we won't."[1] In this speech, Durden pinpoints something that should confront Christians every day—the great depression of a life lived apart from a noble cause. Christians are tempted daily to believe the empty promises of the millionaire, movie-god, and rock-star lifestyles. We are tempted to believe that if we had a little more money, power, notoriety, respect, beauty, influence, or success we would be truly happy. We need to fight to believe in something better. Palahniuk's Fight Club was an attempt to fill a void left by the Church. In an interview he comments, "I started to recognize that, in a way, support groups were becoming the new church of our time—a place where people will go and confess their very worst aspects of their lives and seek redemption and community with outer people in a way that people used to go to church. . . ."[2]

God is calling us to recover and redeem this confessional, redemptive, and communal role of the church. He is calling us out of our depressive, self-centered lives into the rewarding fight of faith, out of the great depression into a great spiritual war. Our spiritual war is a war against the flesh, that lingering vestige of our pre-Christian lives that must be put to death so that we can live in the fullness of life given to us in Jesus (Rom. 8:13). Richard Lovelace describes the flesh as "the fallen human personality apart from the renewing influence and control of the Holy Spirit." He points out that the flesh is more than skin deep. "The New Testament constantly describes it as something much deeper than the isolated moments of sin which it generates. The lists of the works of the flesh in Galatians 5:19–21 and Colossians 3:5-9 point mostly to heart conditions rather than discrete actions."[3] The good news is that we can beat the flesh in the power of the Spirit: *"For if you live according to the flesh you will die, but if by the Spirit you put to death the deeds of the body, you will live"* (Rom. 8:13). This text calls us to fight and "put to death" our sinful patterns of anxiety, self-pity, anger, fear of man, vanity, pride, lust, greed, and every sin we encounter. As we pointed out in chapter 4, these sins are the result of an unbelieving heart or a heart that is motivated by belief in something other than the gospel. When we become disciples of Jesus, we are inducted into a fight club. In this chapter, I will explain the concept of "fight clubs" as a way for all disciples, men and women, to fight for what is truly noble and beautiful. Fight clubs encourage integrated discipleship by focusing attention on the gospel, not piety or mission. My hope is that this approach to discipleship will help you practice gospel holiness while avoiding the extremes of spiritual performance and license. Fight clubs are intended to help us apply the gospel in community in order to reflect the image of Jesus.

What Is a Fight Club?

Fight clubs are small, simple groups of two to three men or women who meet regularly to help one another beat up the flesh and believe the gospel of grace. Men meet with men and women meet with women in order to effectively address gender-specific issues head-on. I have been in fight clubs for years, though I haven't always called them by that name. Some have been better than others. Along the way, I discovered that when the gospel was central to our fighting, these relationships were much more effective in promoting God-honoring discipleship. We "officially" started fight clubs several years ago in our church. They started organically because we didn't want them to compete with the primary community structure (city groups) in our new church plant. There were no sign-ups or classes. I simply preached a sermon on fighting the fight of faith and cast a vision for fight clubs.

People started forming fight clubs right away. I quickly wrote an article to give the groups some guidance. The groups went viral. People started meeting all over the city to fight the fight of faith during the week in bars, coffee shops, and homes. Fight clubs can vary in health and are difficult to monitor, which is a big reason I wrote the original booklet. I wanted to equip our people to fight well with Spirit-empowered faith in the gospel. As the church grew, we occasionally connected people to form a fight club but continued to insist that fight clubs should remain relationally based whenever possible. Good fighting springs from relationships of trust. So how do they work? Three ways: 1) know your sin, 2) fight your sin, 3) trust your Savior.

1. Know Your Sin

First, know your sin. We can know our sin by asking three questions: *What, When,* and *Why*? Consider the *what* first. Before we can fight our sin, we must know what sins are currently present in our lives. An unknown opponent is difficult to defeat. Knowing our sin requires familiarity with our particular temptations, areas where we are prone to sin. These temptations and sins may be visible or invisible, as obvious as anger or as subtle as self-pity. Begin by prayerfully reflecting on your life. Remember, you are God's child, not his project. He knows you and loves you enough to show you your sin. Talk to him about your struggles; ask him to reveal your sins and convict you of them (Ps. 139:23–24; John 16:8). Another way to get at the *what* is to ask your fight club partners to point out sins they see in your life. Very often, we fail to see our own weaknesses. A loving community can help us by holding up the mirror of God's Word so that we can see ourselves more clearly. While community is helpful, the Word is powerful, sharper than any sword, dividing between things visible and invisible, judging the thoughts and intentions of the heart (Heb. 4:12). Use God's Word as a mirror to expose sin and as a sword to convict. Reading through James with my fight club recently helped us grasp our deep need for wisdom. As a result, we embraced God's grace agenda to change us in trial and suffering. Minister to one another with God's Word, not mere opinion. You can know your sin by praying, discussing, and reading the Word in community with a humble, teachable heart.

Once you have identified the *what*, it is important to consider the *when*. When are you tempted to sin? If we don't think about the when, sin will sneak up on us. Consider the circumstances that surround your sin, where and when you find yourself tempted. Identify your sins and the circumstances of temptation. For example:

- Do you find yourself tempted to *vanity* or *self-pity* when lingering in front of the mirror?
- Does sexual *lust* or *despair* creep in on late, lonely nights watching TV?
- Are you prone to *pride* when you succeed or receive a compliment?
- Are you easily *angered* in traffic or while waiting in line?

In order to overcome sin, we have to know what it is and when it creeps up on us. This means thinking about the circumstances of temptation—rejection, compliments, late nights, or standing in front of the mirror. Consider the circumstances of your temptation to know when you sin.

Finally, the critical question to ask in knowing our sin is *why?* The why question is important because it gets to the motivation behind our sin; it addresses the heart. No one ever sins out of duty. We all sin because we want to, because our hearts long for something. If we don't address the motivational issues behind our sin, we will only treat it superficially, adjusting our behavior, not our hearts. God doesn't want mere behavioral adjustment; he wants affectionate obedience! To uncover your motivation, ask yourself why you gravitate to certain sins. What do you believe they will do for you? What is your heart longing for? What are you desiring or valuing most when you sin in a particular area? Using the examples above, we may sin because we desire worth, companionship, peace, confidence, or convenience. These longings are not inherently bad; however, when they are associated with a lie they become deadly. Consider these examples of how good things can be twisted by lies into sinful motivations:

> **Lust**: If you find sexual intimacy on the Internet, then you won't be lonely or stressed.
> **Vanity**: If you perform beautifully, then you have worth.
> **Pride**: If you received more compliments, then you would be more confident.
> **Anger**: If you get angry, you can get your way.

Many of our sins can be traced back to a deep belief in a lie. These false promises of acceptance, approval, satisfaction, self-worth, beauty, and significance motivate our sin.[4] If we are to discover true acceptance, approval, satisfaction, self-worth, beauty, and significance, we need the ability to expose those lies. Cultivate a habit of looking beneath your sin to expose the lie underneath it. We need to get to the lie beneath the sin.[5] Get to the motivational why. Once we understand why we sin, the false promise we believe, we can replace it with a better why, a better promise. If we don't address the why question, we will inevitably become religious or rebellious disciples who just try harder or give up trying altogether. To avoid this, we need a better motivation. We need gospel motivation.[6] Once we have identified our motivation for sinning, we can replace it with a superior gospel motivation. Knowing our sin involves knowing the *what* (sin), the *when* (circumstance), and the *why* (motive). *Know your sin.*

2. Fight Your Sin

Second, fight your sin. Once we know our sin, the challenge is to actually fight it. Before we address fighting sin, it is worthwhile to point out that victory over sin has already been won in Christ. The good news of the gospel is that Jesus has defeated sin, death, and evil through his own death and resurrection and is making all things new, even us. Therefore, the battles we fight against sin take place within a larger war that has already been won. This brings to mind the famous analogy of D-day versus V-day.[7] A war is often effectively won through a decisive battle, though skirmishes and fighting often continue until the final day of victory. D-day occurred in World War II when Allied Forces defeated the Germans at Normandy Beach, where they won both the battle and the war. Although the decisive victory was won at Normandy, battles continued until the armistice was officially signed on V-day, the final day of victory. Similarly,

Jesus won the war over sin, death, and evil in his D-day victory at the cross. He defeated the penalty, power, and presence of sin. We will never bear the penalty of sin because Jesus bore our penalty for us in his wrath-absorbing death. The power of sin has been broken because Jesus has given us new life. The presence of sin will be eternally banished once we die or are united with Jesus in his return. Paul explains Jesus's victory over sin and its implications for us in Romans 6:

> We know that our old self was crucified with him in order that the body of sin might be brought to nothing, so that we would no longer be enslaved to sin. For one who has died has been set free from sin. Now if we have died with Christ, we believe that we will also live with him. We know that Christ, being raised from the dead, will never die again; death no longer has dominion over him. For the death he died he died to sin, once for all, but the life he lives he lives to God. So you also must consider yourselves dead to sin and alive to God in Christ Jesus. (vv. 6–11)

The power of sin has been rendered powerless, as we are no longer enslaved to it but to Christ! However, disciples continue to battle sin until the V-day arrives in our final reunion with Christ. This is why Paul exhorts us to "consider" ourselves dead to sin and alive in Jesus. The time between D-day (the cross) and V-day (the return of Christ) will be filled with battles against sin, but in these battles we possess a new life which enables us to defeat sin through Christ's decisive victory. The fight of faith is a fight to be our new, authentic selves in Christ, free from sin and alive to God in righteousness. Knowing our sin, we fight against it by fighting to be who we already are in Christ.

Our skirmishes against sin arise from an attitude of the

heart. Fighting sin is a tenacity to put it to death, which arises from our life in Christ. Unfortunately, many disciples do not walk in their newness of life but in old patterns of sin. Perhaps this lackadaisical approach to sin is because we value Jesus's atonement for our guilt and the penalty of sin, but at a heart level we fail to value and understand how his atonement has also freed us from the power of sin? Or perhaps our indifference to fighting sin springs from a false belief that God accepts us just as we are, not as who we will be? Why fight if we are already accepted? However, if we are accepted not as we are but as we are in Christ, we have every reason to fight—from our new identity. The truth is, persistent, unrepentant sin can disqualify us from the kingdom of God (Gal. 5:19–21; Eph. 5:5; Heb. 3:7–13). God does not accept us as we are. He accepts us as we are in Christ. In him, we are a new creation (2 Cor. 5:17; Gal. 6:15), and new creatures live transformed (not perfect) lives. As recipients of God's grace, we are compelled to follow Jesus in all of life.[8] We will fight to find Jesus sweeter, richer, deeper, and more satisfying than anything else in the world. Disciples contend with their sin because they love their Savior.

Mortification of Sin

In my discipleship, the writings of John Owen continue to be tremendously helpful. Owen's books, *Of the Mortification of Sin* and *On Temptation*, are classics on the subject of fighting sin. In his preface to *Of the Mortification of Sin* (*mortification* is an old word meaning "to put to death"), Owen articulates the purpose for writing on the subject: "That mortification and universal holiness may be promoted in my own and in the hearts and ways of others, to the glory of God; so that the gospel of our

Lord and Saviour Jesus Christ may be adorned in all things."[9] Mortification is that tenacious disposition of the heart that longs to defeat sin out of love for Jesus. Notice that Owen sets mortification of sin in its rightful place, not as an end in itself, but as a means to making much of the gospel of Christ. Owen keeps the gospel, not fighting, central to discipleship, while retaining an appropriate tenacity in fighting our relentless foe. He writes: "Be killing sin lest it be killing you."[10] Paul issues similar injunctions:

- "*Put to death* therefore what is earthly in you: sexual immorality, impurity, passion, evil desire, and covetousness, which is idolatry. On account of these the wrath of God is coming." (Col. 3:5–6)
- "For if you live according to the flesh you will die, but if by the Spirit you *put to death* the deeds of the body, you will live." (Rom. 8:13)
- "*Take care, brothers, lest there be in any of you an evil, unbelieving heart*, leading you to fall away from the living God. But exhort one another every day, as long as it is called 'today,' that none of you may be hardened by the deceitfulness of sin." (Heb. 3:12–13)

Sin is no lighthearted matter. It is crouching at our door and we must master it (Gen. 4:7). It is dangerous to not fight sin. It is a sobering fight that must not cease. *Fight your sin* means a habitual weakening of the flesh through constant fighting and contending in the Spirit for sweet victory over sin. It should be regular and progressive, not occasional and instant. Fighting is not an end in itself or a way to make us more presentable to God. We fight because we have been made presentable in Christ. We fight for belief in his gospel, the truest and best news on earth—that Jesus has defeated our sin, death, and evil through his own death and resurrection, and he is making all things new, even us. Until all things are new, we will continue to fight the good fight of faith.

Fight club is ultimately about life, not death—about joy, not sorrow. It is about the gospel, not good works. We don't fight for acceptance; we fight from our acceptance. We don't contend against sin to forge an identity but because we have received a new identity in Christ. Perfection is not the goal; persevering faith is. As my former seminary professor Scott Hafemann used to say: "It's not perfection overnight but perseverance over a lifetime."[11] *Fight your sin.*

3. Trust Your Savior

Third, trust your Savior. This is the best part of discipleship. Trusting our Savior makes discipleship personal. Discipleship isn't a program or a one-on-one meeting. It is fundamentally a trusting relationship with Jesus based on his gospel of grace. When we trust in his promises, we cut through religious performance and spiritual license, leading to soul-sweetening obedience. When we trust Jesus, we displace rules from the center of our discipleship and replace it with his gospel. The fight against sin will fade once and for all, but we will trust our Savior forever. Why not begin closing the gap now? He is utterly trustworthy—the same yesterday, today, and forever (Heb. 13:8). All God's promises are "Yes" and "Amen" in him (2 Cor. 1:20). The trouble, of course, is that we are adept at displacing the gospel from our discipleship and replacing it with rules.

My wife met Michael's wife in a local bookstore. Over time, we got to know this couple through parties and meals in our home. Eventually they began participating in more formal church gatherings like our city groups and Sundays. They heard gospel preaching regularly. I remember seeing a copy of *Fight Clubs* (a booklet version of this book) in Michael's hand. He was reading gospel literature and participating in gospel community. Curious as to how much he had absorbed, I asked him out to lunch. After catching up and hearing about his struggle to provide for his family, I asked Michael: "How are things with Jesus?" Michael responded by telling me about a man at work whom he considered his "moral superior." He went on to say: "I'm no saint but I'm climbing the spiritual ladder." After affirming his struggle to provide for his family, I asked him if I could pick out a couple of things that he mentioned and discuss them with him. Referring to his "moral superior" at work, I told Michael: "Unfortunately, you'll never be moral enough and you will never measure up to a holy God. In fact, no matter how high you climb the spiritual ladder, you'll never reach him. But there is good news. Jesus actually climbed down the spiritual ladder for you, died for your failure to perform morally, rose again, placed you on his back, and then climbed back up the spiritual ladder, where he placed you right in the presence of a holy God, fully loved and fully accepted. That, Michael, is what Jesus has to do with your life." Michael wasn't trusting the Savior. He was trusting himself. When I finished speaking, I asked Michael what he thought. With a joyful glow on his face, he looked at me and said: "Oh, is it really that easy?" To which I responded: "Yes, Michael, it really is that easy. That's what it means to trust Jesus."

Many of us are like Michael. Discipleship is moral, not personal. We depersonalize the gospel by removing Jesus and replacing him with our own efforts. When the Spirit is a forgotten god, trusting Jesus becomes a fading proposition. He is present in name only. Jesus becomes an idea we believe, not a person we trust. Consequently, religious affection and the power of the Spirit leak out. Doubt and cynicism roll in. Discipleship devolves into dutiful performance. Instead of trusting Jesus's finished work, we begin to rely on our own work to overcome sin. Eventually, frustration, despair, and anger set it. Before we know it, we will swing to the religious right or the rebellious left, trusting our own performance or the deceptive rush of spiritual license. Everyone trusts something or someone; the gospel reminds us that only one person is worthy of our trust.

Trusting the Word and the Spirit

How, then, do we trust our Savior? We trust his personal Word to us. We take him at his word. We fight to believe in what God has promised us in Jesus (2 Cor. 1:20). Faith comes, not from mustering it up, but through reliance on the Holy Spirit. Reliance on the Spirit isn't a method or special prayer; it is a relationship of dependence upon him. It's communion with God. The Spirit is the presence and power of God to help us trust our Savior. The Spirit empowers faith in the Word of God. Romans 8:13 reminds us of the role of the Spirit in our fight to trust Jesus: "For if you live according to the flesh you will die, but if *by the Spirit* you put to death the deeds of the body, you will live." We are to fight in a particular way—*by the Spirit*. The Spirit inclines our hearts to believe the promises of God. He does not incline us to believe false promises such as: the promises of vanity to have worth, self-pity to rectify poor self-image, sexual lust for intimacy, or anger to get our way. The Spirit wants to empower us to believe better promises, promises that are true and lasting. When faced with temptation, the part of us that leans away from sin and toward Jesus is the Spirit of

God. Yield to him. Don't make temptation an inner dialogue with your reason; make it an opportunity to commune with the Spirit. Surrender to his promptings. Be yourself in Christ, and turn to God's promises in faith.

Practical Trust in God

Surrendering to the Spirit to trust the Son may seem vague or impractical. How can we practically rely upon the Spirit to trust the Savior? By the Word and the Spirit of God. The Spirit works through the Word. Like lightning works through steel, the Spirit's power is released through Scripture to awaken our hearts to the glory of God dazzling off the face of Christ. The Spirit was given freely to us for understanding and faith in God's Word: "Now we have received not the spirit of the world, but the Spirit who is from God, that we might understand the things freely given us by God" (1 Cor. 2:12). Those things freely given to us by God are, indeed, his precious and magnificent promises. In order to trust Jesus, we need to know his promises. More specifically, we need to know promises and warnings that address our personal temptations and trials. Fumes from Sunday worship are not enough for the fight of faith. We need the sword of truth by our side and the Spirit of God inside to draw the Word at a moment's notice. If we are to fight for the joyous image of Christ to be revealed in us, we need to read God's Word regularly.

Cultivating Fresh Faith in the Gospel

How do we cultivate Bible reading that brings us fresh faith in the gospel? To be honest, there are times that old, memorized promises don't always work for me. Is this because "trusting your Savior" doesn't work? No, it's because my heart becomes indifferent to them. How do we revive our hearts to take interest in God's promises? John Owen recommends we return to prayer, but perhaps not as you usually pray. He notes that if we wisely consider the Spirit's working *in* our hearts by prayer, we may understand much of his working *upon* our hearts by grace. In order to have fresh faith in the gospel, we ought to pray to the Spirit for three things: 1) insight into his promises, 2) experience of our need, 3) creation of desire.[12] All too often we assume the insight, neglect to experience our need, and are too proud to ask for desire.

What if, whenever we read the Bible and felt as though we got nothing out of it, we paused to ask the Spirit for *insight into God's promises*, to ask him, "Lord, you have been given to us so that we can understand all the things freely given to us by God. Will you give me insight into God's Word right now?" Have you ever gained an insight in Scripture but not known how to respond? What if, instead of trying to figure out application on our own, we asked the Spirit to give us an *experience of our need*? Pause to ask him: "Lord, who knows the heart of man like the Spirit of God, will you help me to experience my specific need for God right now?" Perhaps the Spirit will lead you to respond by rejoicing, repenting, or obeying. Finally, have you ever read with insight, known your need, but felt no desire to respond to God? Don't move on or assume you will have the proper response. Pause and ask the Spirit: "Lord, forgive me for my lack of desire, and create fresh, new desire in me to respond to Jesus." Ask the Spirit to give you insight into his promises, an experience of your need, and a desire to respond. Approach God's Word with God's Spirit. Plead for the lightning while carrying the rod, and ask the Spirit for these three things to revive an indifferent heart.

Gospel Homework

As you read God's Word, take confidence that the Spirit longs to give you fresh insight into God's promises. Begin doing gospel homework by looking for promises of grace to rebuff the promises of sin. Look for the Lord's instruction regarding the what, why, and when of your sin. Develop a practice of identifying the promises of sin against the promises of Christ. For example:

Sexual Lust: The Fight for True Intimacy

- Instead of trusting sexual lust for intimacy, trust God for true intimacy: *"Blessed are the pure in heart, for they shall see God"* (Matt. 5:8). When you are tempted to lust, turn to God's promise for true intimacy, to see God and be ravished with him in Jesus.

  > **Lust** says: "Long for what you cannot have and you will be happy."

  > **The gospel** says: "Rejoice in what you do have, in Jesus, and you will be truly happy."

Vanity: The Fight for True Worth

- Instead of relying on vanity for worth, consider the beauty of God: *"What we will be has not yet appeared; but we know that when he appears we shall be like him, because we shall see him as he is"* (1 John 3:2). When you are tempted to find your worth in your appearance, turn to God's beauty and rest in the beauty you have in him.

  > **Vanity** says: "Perform beautifully and you will have worth."

  > **The gospel** says: "Jesus performed beautifully for you; therefore, you have never-ending worth."

Pride: The Fight for True Confidence

- Instead of trusting in compliments for confidence, believe that your sufficiency comes from God: *"Such is the confidence that we have through Christ toward God. Not that we are sufficient in ourselves to claim anything as coming from us, but our sufficiency is from God, who has made us sufficient"* (2 Cor. 3:4–6).

> **Pride** says: "Find and cherish compliments and then you will be confident."
>
> **The gospel** says: "Your confidence comes, not from your sufficiency, but from God who has made you sufficient in Jesus."

Anger: The Fight for God's Way

- Instead of getting angry to get your way (protesting not getting your way), put your trust in the Lord's way: "Be angry, and do not sin; ponder in your own hearts on your beds, and be silent. Offer right sacrifices, and put your trust in the LORD" (Ps. 4:4–5).

> **Anger** says: "If I control my circumstances (and I have a right to) then I will get the best outcome. If I can't control my circumstances, then I have the right to get mad."
>
> **The gospel** says: "Because Jesus is Lord, he has the right to control my circumstances. Therefore, I will get the best outcome by trusting him. Put your trust in the Lord, not in controlling your circumstances."

Get in the habit of comparing the promises of sin to the promises of the gospel. I have found it incredibly helpful to write down a sin promise next to a gospel promise in order to see the staggering difference between the two. When you identify the sin promise, it forces you to search the Scriptures for *how the gospel offers a better promise.* There's something about seeing the futility of sin next to the beauty of Christ. Make a habit of doing gospel homework and looking for grace in God's promises. Memorize the answers. Quote them to temptation. Write them on your heart. Most importantly, believe gospel promises and encourage others to do so. This is how we can trust our Savior.

Interestingly, mortification commands come with a promise.

If we *"put to death the deeds of the body,"* then we will live (Rom. 8:13). This promised life is eternal life, life that begins with faith in Christ and endures for eternity (Rom. 8:10–11). Those who trust in the resurrected Christ for eternal life will receive immortal bodies in which they will enjoy God and his renewed creation forever. No more sin, suffering, or fighting! The greatest weapon against sin and temptation is Spirit-empowered faith in the promises of God, which have been guaranteed by the death of Christ. Don't trust the fleeting promises of sin. Trust in the promises of your Savior.

How Does a Fight Club Work?

How can we apply these principles while practicing the three conversions? I recommend forming discipleship relationships of trust around the three gospel principles. Commit to God and to one another that you will apply these principles to yourselves and to one another. We do this in what we call fight clubs. You can call them fight clubs, something different, or nothing at all. What matters is that you are fighting for faith in the gospel with other disciples. Fight clubs are simple, reproducible, missional, and biblical. *Simple*: There are no more than two to three people to a group gathering in the ordinary rhythms of life (breakfast, lunch, an evening out) to encourage one another in the gospel. *Reproducible*: If the group grows beyond three, it is important that the newest member participates only a couple of times to get the idea and then starts a new group. This retains the intimacy and trust built in the initial group, while also fostering reproduction—more fight clubs! *Missional*: In order to maintain missional discipleship, make a practice of sharing your stories and conversations with non-Christians and pray for them together. *Biblical*: Fight clubs are simple and biblical in their content. I recommend reading the Bible together and following a progression of *Text-Theology-Life*.

Text-Theology-Life

Text-Theology-Life is essentially how I read the Bible and teach others how to interpret it. This is a simplified explanation of what I usually take two months to teach in our church. If you haven't read a book or taken a class on Bible interpretation (also known as hermeneutics), I highly recommend doing so.[13] This will help you read the Bible in context and with Christ-centered understanding, which is critical to cultivating gospel holiness.

Text: I recommend that your fight club read the same biblical text together during the week. If the Bible isn't central, you will end up relying on yourself and one another. You will find it difficult to get past conversations about life. However, if the Bible is central, you will be more likely to respond to God and rely on the gospel. Each person should commit to reading the same chapter from a book of the Bible each week. For example, your group could read through Colossians in four weeks, taking one chapter a week. As you read, make a point of asking the Holy Spirit to draw your attention to what he wants to accomplish in you. The Spirit may be prompting you to repent of a sin, rejoice in a promise, meditate on an insight, or praise God for an attribute. Each week, when you get together, make the text your initial focus by sharing how the Spirit has moved through the Word to change you.

Theology: Moving from text to theology, work through the text in community, trying to follow the flow of the author. From there, try to understand the central theological message of the chapter. Ask yourself: "Where is the gospel reflected in this text?"

The gospel is always in context. When your sinful doubts, fears, and desires are surfaced by the text, discern your ungodly motivations and redress them with gospel motivations present in the passage. Identify your belief in false promises, repent, and turn to trust in God's good and true promises. Strive to be Christ centered, not application centered. The goal is not to "apply" the text but to be awestruck with Jesus, not to "do" but to delight in him. Then, from our delight in Christ and our belief in his promises, we can apply the gospel to everyday temptations and trials. Make Jesus central. For every look at sin look ten times at Christ!

Life: As you move from theology to life, inject your life struggles and successes into the conversation. Allow plenty of time for this. Ask one another questions. Graciously press one another to discern ungodly motivations and get to gospel motivations. This is not a Bible study; it is a fight club. Share your lives, not just your insights. Adorn the gospel by confessing sin and repenting well. Remember, Christ alone is sufficient for your failures and strong for your successes. Take it all to the Lord Jesus in faithful prayer for one another, on the spot, not just afterward. Finally, be sure to share the names of people you are trying to bless with the gospel. Pray as a group, asking God to help you trust his promises as well as to give unbelievers in your lives the very same gift of faith!

Gospel Principles Applied in My Fight Club

My current fight club meets every other Friday. We typically meet at a quiet coffee shop for an hour and half. As friends, we will reconnect briefly and then jump into an issue or the reading. Sometimes our gathering is powerful and sometimes it isn't. Sometimes we miss due to travel or holidays, but taking the marathon approach, we've seen God work in and through each of us to make one another more like Jesus. Sometimes I am the one who asks questions that get us deeper into the gospel. This isn't always the case. I've had fight clubs where my friends asked those questions just as much. This may take time as the natural leader leads out. However, we all need to learn to ask deep and pinpointed questions in order expose sin and make room for grace to seep down into our hearts. This practice takes time. It's important for disciples to agree to live by gospel principles while also keeping expectations of one another reasonable.

When my fight club read through James, I remember being challenged to cultivate biblical wisdom. It was an aha! moment, when I realized that wisdom isn't becoming an old guy with just the right thing to say, but instead, becoming a person who pleads with God to change me into the image of his Son, whatever the circumstances of life (James 1:2–8; 3:13–18). Here are a couple snapshots of "becoming wise" in one of our fight club meetings.

In a recent meeting, we read and discussed chapter drafts of this book. When we read chapter 2, one person asked: "Where do you guys lean, toward vertical or horizontal discipleship?" It was a great question (I recommend asking it). I responded by saying that, at different times in my life, I have leaned toward one or the other. I described my piety-centered discipleship as a college student. As I talked, it became apparent to me that my collegiate focus on piety was a silent way to atone for my moral failures as a Christian. Although I read the Bible, fasted, and prayed with genuine desire for God, I also hoped that I would regain his approval through my religious performance. After all, I had an annulment, slept with a few women, and was kicked out of Bible school. This pious self-atonement was entirely unconscious.

Eventually, I reached a breaking point in my early twenties. I recall sitting in the driver's seat of my little Dodge Colt, slumped over, ridden with guilt, and weeping over my sexual failures. I straightened up with spiritual resolve. I would no longer heap shame on the name of Christ. With my pocketknife open and in hand, I would end my life and cease to sin. I pressed the knife against my flesh, on my wrist, so I would die. No more dishonor, no more shame. Religious performance will be the end of you. Trusting in your morality, or living a life of rebellious immorality, will be the end of you unless you turn from sin to trust your Savior. That Savior is Jesus. My fight club helped me interpret my past with the gospel by asking me good questions.

Truth be told, that day Jesus saved me for the billionth time. His gospel is always saving us because nothing else can, not even for a moment. Jesus shed his blood so that we don't have to. Instead of death, God gives us life, a life worth living. God restrained my hand, and turned me, once again, to Christ. Although I didn't realize it at the time, God was showering me with grace. He was teaching me the gospel. He was saying: "Jonathan, my Son has already performed for all your moral failures. His perfect death on the cross has washed away all your past, present, and future sins. His victorious resurrection has liberated you from the power of sin and given you new life. His gift of the Spirit will lead you into a life of repentance and faith in the gospel. That will honor me, not a perfect moral track record. I do want your devotion, but I don't want your performance." Belief in the gospel will save your life again and again and again.

I turned the question about discipleship leanings back onto one of my friends. He shared how he struggles with vertical discipleship. He confessed that, very often, he feels like a failure if he doesn't spend enough time in sermon preparation. I asked him if he thought that was from God. He confessed it wasn't, and that it was a lie he had believed for some time, a religious lie that was debilitating. It overflowed into his prayer life. Failing to pray or make it through a prayer list left him feeling inferior. This too was a lie. As we talked, we witnessed repentance. It was powerful, sincere, and gospel centered. I said something like: "God doesn't want your well-prepared sermons; he wants you." I tried to encourage him by pointing out that we are all inferior, but that God makes all of us sufficient in the gospel. I referred to 2 Cor. 3:5–6: "Not that we are sufficient in ourselves to claim anything as coming from us, but our sufficiency is from God, who has made us sufficient *to be ministers of a new covenant.*" I emphasized God's qualifying work in the Spirit to be a minister, a pastor, a disciple. We asked questions that opened him up so the gospel of grace could flow down into the crevices of his heart. The next Friday meeting, my friend had to do some unexpected counseling, a funeral, and had just returned from a conference. Sermon preparation was not in order. I said something like: "Tell your people you've been so busy being a great pastor that they will have to settle for a good or okay sermon. Don't overprepare or beat yourself up. Just give them the gospel." He received it and not only preached the gospel but also preached from the gospel. Pastors need the very same thing every other disciple needs, the gospel of grace. They need to be reminded, challenged, confronted, and exhorted in grace. Every disciple needs relationships with people who will commit to helping one another keep Jesus in the middle of their discipleship.

Fight clubs are simple, reproducible, missional, and biblical, following the pattern of Text-Theology-Life. They avoid religious performance by promoting a Christ-centered reading of the Scriptures and gospel-centered motivation for discipleship. They avoid spiritual license by taking seriously the fight of faith. Best of all, they promote lasting joy in Jesus and, as a result, adorn his glorious gospel. When we apply the gospel in community by knowing our sin, fighting our sin, and trusting our Savior, sin is defeated and Christ is exalted. We obey Jesus as Lord and repent to Jesus as Christ. This is not a one-and-done. It is a way to apply an everyday gospel to everyday challenges within the community God has given us. When we gather around the gospel, not breaking or keeping rules, we discover just how incomparable the gospel of Jesus truly is.

8

GOSPEL-CENTERED CULTURE: MATURING AND MULTIPLYING DISCIPLES

Now that you have read most of the book, you're wondering how you can start a fight club? How can churches and ministries promote and maintain healthy, gospel-centered disciples? How should fight clubs fit into the overall structure of your church or ministry? This chapter will address these questions and more in order to help you create a gospel-centered culture that makes and matures gospel-centered disciples.

How to Start a Fight Club

It's easy to start a fight club. Here are a few tips to observe when starting one.

Choose Your Fight Club Partners

Fight clubs are relationally driven, so pick people you can trust. Establish an agreed-upon level of confidentiality within your group. Make a commitment to one another. Fight clubs of uncommitted people simply don't promote gospel-centered fighting.

Read the Book

People who don't read the book don't fight well. They end up reinforcing legalism or license. Reading the book will get you on the same page, so you can fight sin with faith in the gospel! We recommend reading a chapter a week and discussing it, so you can pursue gospel-centered discipleship together.

Set a Regular Meeting Time

One of the first things you should do is sync your calendars for a regular meeting time. If you don't schedule a regular meeting time, you won't meet regularly. Meet once a week or every other week. Allow at least an hour.

How to Keep the Gospel Central

I frequently get asked how to keep the gospel central in fight clubs. My first answer is to emphasize the gospel over religious performance and spiritual license. People are typically looking for a best practice, but this point cannot be emphasized enough. If your church or ministry doesn't emphasize the centrality of the gospel in everyday life, then your disciples will make other things central such as community, mission, convenience, comfort, and legalism. Reinforce gospel-centered DNA in your ministry in as many ways as possible (modeling, stories, counseling, sermons, articles, blogs, books, tweets, and trainings). Another way to do this is to publically address discipleship pitfalls from the pulpit or stage. Remind people that fight clubs can turn into gossip clubs, cheap grace clubs, legalism clubs, or nonexistent clubs if they don't remain focused on the gospel. Show them how and why the gospel leads to different, deeper, richer discipleship.

Talk about fight clubs as an integral part of your church. Do this when you cast vision for the church, when you make application in messages, and through your website and social media. This will remind people how important it is to practice the three gospel conversions to Christ, church, and mission. Encourage fight club stories and conversations to be shared from the stage and in your small groups. This encourages practical trust in Jesus and spreads desire to believe the gospel. Develop practical gospel language that people can use to disciple one another. I have noticed that our collective effort in discipleship overflows in the creation of helpful phrases. It is not unusual to hear people in our church say things like:

"God is good, all the time."
"Are you fighting well?"
"What lie might you be believing?"
"How is Jesus better?"
"Are you having fresh encounters with Christ?"
"What are you learning about the gospel?"

Gospel phrases and questions can be very helpful, but nothing replaces first-hand Bible reading. A final way to promote gospel-centered discipleship is for groups to meet regularly. Those that meet regularly experience much deeper gospel change. Groups that do not set a regular meeting time or meet only when it's convenient struggle to get off the ground and to remain centered on Jesus. Meeting at least every other week is key.

How to Implement Fight Clubs

It is important to continually promote fight clubs in your church body if they are to become an effective part of your discipleship ministry. For fight clubs to take root, your community must know what they are and how they work. The best way to launch them is through the leaders of a ministry. After leaders have read and begun this gospel-centered approach to discipleship, they can communicate the process of fight clubs to everyone else. Pastors sometimes do this through Sunday sermons or weekend seminars. Some ministry leaders have introduced fight clubs through a weekly meeting, weekend retreat, or conference. Here are a few more things we have found helpful in making disciples through fight clubs.

Tell Stories

Stories connect people to the need for fight clubs and encourage them to join one. Tell stories of how fight clubs have helped people fight sin and trust Jesus. Stories will breathe life and health into your groups by providing concrete examples of gospel-centered discipleship. This can happen in a variety of settings. One of our pastors shared how his fight club was instrumental in helping him through a very difficult time in his marriage. These men helped him when he needed help most. They pointed him away from despair and to the hope of redemption in Christ. They encouraged him through a difficult season by regularly speaking the gospel into his life, texting him Scriptures, and praying for him. When our pastor shared this, couples took great encouragement in their own marriages from this fight club story and still talk about it.

Read and Reread the Book

Encourage your people to read and reread the book. We ask our fight clubs to read *Gospel-Centered Discipleship* every few months so that they continue to fight sin with faith in the promises of God. Also, take advantage of the free gospel-centered resources online at www.gospelcentereddiscipleship.com.

Equipping Resources

Seminars are great way to inspire, equip, and encourage disciples in the gospel. Host a seminar on a Saturday morning, eat breakfast, share stories, and teach how the gospel can be central in fighting sin. This strengthens people as you inject good, practical gospel DNA into the body of Christ. I have spoken at conferences on gospel-centered discipleship to assist local churches in launching fight clubs in their churches. There are more and more churches implementing this approach to discipleship, so check our website to find out what other churches are doing. On this note, New Life Church has enlisted fight club coaches who oversee one to three groups to provide additional support and counsel for their groups. Pastor Rick White at CityView Church says that their fight clubs went on steroids after starting redemption groups. Mike Wilkerson describes a redemption group as "an intense small group that digs deep into difficult and seldom-discussed areas of life, such as abuse, addiction, and trials of all sorts."[1] At CityView, they discovered that redemption groups furnished his church with language and significant heart change to fuel fight clubs. Rick notes: "I consider Redemption Groups, in many ways, 'reactive' discipleship while Fight Clubs allow us to become 'proactive' in discipling one another."[2]

Church after church stresses the importance of continuing to emphasize the gospel in their overall ministries. Fight clubs are not a program. They are an expression of gospel-centered ministry by and for disciples of Jesus. However, treating them as a panacea for discipleship will backfire. The only cure for legalism and license among disciples is the gospel, not fight clubs. Whatever you do, make sure that the gospel is the answer, but be sure to show one another *how* the gospel is the answer.

Frequently Asked Questions

1. Can I call them something different from fight clubs?

Of course! Just don't call them "cat fights" when forming them for women! What matters most is men and women getting together regularly, not just for small talk but for gospel talk. Call them whatever you like, just be sure to keep faith in Jesus and his promises central. Cultivate friendships that encourage religious affection, repentance and faith, and deep dependence on the Holy Spirit.

2. How long should fight clubs be committed to one another?

Because they are based on friendships, fight clubs should be indefinite. They are selective relationships of trust gathered around Jesus that should endure. This does not mean that they will be free from difficulty, pain, and mess. I have watched fight clubs try to split up over personality or sin issues. Jesus calls us to do precisely the opposite (Matthew 18), to go to one another and be reconciled. Tension in relationships is God's appointed grace for our gospel change. To leave a fight club without addressing the conflict or underlying issue is to depart from God's grace. You may have to have a "fight club" over fight club! Another reason your partners might change is if a fight club will need to multiply for the sake of creating new groups and spreading more gospel. Some people in our church are multiplying fight clubs very intentionally to make disciples.

3. What challenges have you faced in implementing fight clubs?

- Twisted motives: The default mode of the heart (legalism and license) is an unflagging challenge in gospel-centered discipleship. As a disciple, it is important to exhort, encourage, teach, pray, and equip one another for gospel-centered living. Never weary of it. It is your life's calling.

- Messy discipleship: It gets messy when people get deep and close. Be prepared for a spike in counseling support, and don't be afraid to ask other mentors, counselors, or pastors in your church to help you through your trials. Gospel holiness is not restricted to a fight club. In fact, fight club conversations should occur in your small groups as you seek gospel holiness with your entire community.

- Bible-less groups: People tend to slip off from making the Bible (Text-Theology-Life) central in fight club meetings. When this happens, they end up relying on secondhand gospel sayings or old Bible verses, not fresh words from the Spirit and belief in the promises of God. When this happens, the gospel loses its center of gravity and discipleship becomes dutiful. Don't change the order of your fight club to Life-Theology-Text by starting with your life! You will rarely get to the Bible and encounter fresh power of the Spirit working through God's Word to change you. Start with the Word. Keep it central, and allow it to shape your life, not your life dictate your time.

4. How do fight clubs work for pastors?

Every pastor should be in a peer, gospel-centered, discipleship relationship. This enables him to effectively watch his life and doctrine closely. If he does, he will save both himself and his hearers (1 Tim. 4:16). I meet with two other pastors every other Friday. I am as transparent as possible with them about my life and struggle to believe the gospel. They have been a source of regular encouragement and correction for me. I occasionally share my fight club experiences with our staff. I practice a similar level of transparency with our church, but with discernment. Everyone in your church doesn't need to know your every struggle; that is what a fight club is for! In practicing pastoral transparency, I have found Matt Chandler's advice helpful. He tells people that they can't earn their way into close relationships with pastors, but they can earn their way out. Good counsel.

In conclusion, this book is not about creating a fight club culture. It is about gospel-centered culture, being and making gospel-centered disciples who fight to live all of life under the redemptive reign of Jesus Christ. This kind of disciple fights for image—to be transformed into the image of Christ with ever-increasing glory, which comes from the Lord, who is the Spirit (2 Cor. 3:18). Religious legalism and spiritual license are set against this glorious purpose. Therefore, we must fight to keep Jesus, not rules, central to our discipleship.

Fortunately, God has given us everything we need in the gospel of Jesus Christ—religious affection, promises and warnings, repentance and faith. Most of all, he has given us himself in the presence and power of his Spirit, who is the motivation behind the motivation. He has made us new creatures in Christ so that we can walk out the implications of the gospel in everyday life.

The fight to be a gospel-centered disciple is noble and glorious but cannot be fought alone. We have been converted not only to Christ but also to one another. The lordship of Christ is most visible in his interdependent body, not a loose collection of disciples. This community of disciples is intended to encourage faith in Jesus and joyfully embrace the call to gospel holiness. These disciples band together to know their sin, fight their sin, and trust their Savior by repenting from faith in false promises and returning to faith in true promises we obey Jesus as Lord and repent to him as Christ. When we do this, we put Jesus at the center of our lives, drawing attention to his grace and glory.

Praying for not-yet Christians and sharing with them how the gospel has changed our lives makes our discipleship missional. We become disciples who not only believe the gospel but also spread it.

Fight clubs are simple, biblical, and missional, a relational way to make and mature gospel-centered disciples. If fight clubs help you make the gospel central, then great. Call them whatever you like or don't call them anything at all, but join with other disciples in making and maturing disciples who trust Jesus. Go with the gospel, learn the gospel, and share the gospel. Go in the power of the gospel, baptize in the grace of the gospel, and teach the Person of the gospel. Jesus is the ground of our going, the goal of our baptizing, and the gospel of our teaching. Gospel-centered discipleship is Jesus-centered discipleship, and Jesus will be with us always, even to the end of the age (Matt. 28:20).

Until we learn to meet him face to face, may we learn the gospel, relate in the gospel, and share the gospel with ever-increasing devotion.

EPILOGUE

One day the fight will be over. Faith will become sight. Our image will be perfectly aligned with Christ's image. Our affection for Christ will be so strong that it *will* be chief among ten thousand. All competitors for his attention will bow before him, and we will recover a childish yet mature delight that will never cease to thrill our souls. Every act will be a natural act of obedience sparked by joy. The warnings will fade and the promises will be fulfilled. Threats will no longer be necessary and rewards will abound. The Spirit will have full sway in our gladdened hearts as we live forever in Spirit-led worship. We will no longer lean toward performance or license. The gospel will be central forever. Our conversions will be complete, our community characterized by love, and our mission colored in with worship. We will no longer know our sin, fight our sin, or struggle to trust our Savior. Until then, may God grant us his sovereign grace to fight the good fight of faith, for our joy and for his eternal glory.

Appendix 1

GOSPEL-CENTERED QUESTIONS TO ASK

Here is a list of questions to help you cultivate gospel motivations. Questions 11–15 are taken from Sam Storms's book, *A Sincere and Pure Devotion to Christ.*[1] See endnote 4 in Chapter 7 for forty-five more questions in David Powlison's list of "X-ray Questions."

What do you desire more than anything else?

What do you find yourself daydreaming or fantasizing about?

What lies do you subtly believe that undermine the truth of the gospel?

Are you astonished with the gospel?

Where have you made much of yourself and little of God?

Is technology interrupting your communion with God?

Is work a source of significance? How?

Where do your thoughts drift when you enter a social setting?

What fears keep you from resting in Christ?

What consumes your thoughts when you have alone time?

When people see how you spend money, do they conclude that God is a priceless treasure, exceedingly valuable above all worldly goods?

When people observe your relationship with others, are they alerted to the power of Christ's forgiveness of you that alone accounts for your forgiveness of them?

If you are complimented for some accomplishment, does the way you receive it drive onlookers to give thanks to the Lord?

Is your use of leisure time or devotion to a hobby or how you speak of your spouse the sort that persuades others that your heart is content with what God is for you in Christ?

Does your reaction to bad news produce in you doubt or fear, or does it inspire confidence to trust in God's providence?

Appendix 2

GOSPEL-CENTERED RESOURCES

Here is a brief list of helpful gospel-centered resources:

Chester, Tim. *You Can Change: God's Transforming Power for Our Sinful Behavior and Negative Emotions.* Wheaton, IL, Crossway, 2010.

Driscoll, Mark, and Gerry Breshears. *Death by Love: Letters from the Cross.* Wheaton, IL: Crossway, 2008.

Keller, Timothy. *Counterfeit Gods: The Empty Promises of Money, Sex, and Power, and the Only Hope that Matters.* New York: Dutton, 2009.

_____. *Prodigal God: Recovering the Heart of the Christian Faith*, New York: Penguin, 2008.

Lane, Timothy S., and Paul David Tripp. *How People Change.* Greensboro, NC: New Growth Press, 2008.

Lovelace, Richard. *Dynamics of Spiritual Life: An Evangelical Theology of Renewal.* Downers Grove, IL: InterVarsity, 1979.

_____. *Renewal as a Way of Life: A Guidebook to Spiritual Growth.* Eugene, OR: Wipf & Stock, 2002.

Lundgaard, Kris. *The Enemy Within: Straight Talk about the Power and Defeat of Sin.* Phillipsburg, NJ: P&R, 1998.

Owen, John. *Mortification of Sin in Believers.* General Books LLC, 2009. http://general-books.net/search.cfm?keyword=Mortification+of+Sin +in+Believers%2C+Owen.

Piper, John. *Future Grace.* Sisters, OR: Multnomah, 2005.

_____. *When I Don't Desire God: How to Fight for Joy.* Wheaton, IL: Crossway, 2004.

Smallman, Stephen. *The Walk: Steps for New and Renewed Followers of Jesus.* Phillipsburg, NJ: P&R, 2009.

Tchividjian, Tullian. *Jesus + Nothing = Everything.* Wheaton, IL: Crossway, 2011.

Thorn, Joe. *Note to Self: The Discipline of Preaching to Yourself.* Wheaton, IL: Crossway, 2011.

Thune, Bob, and Will Walker. *The Gospel-Centered Life: A Nine-Lesson Study.* Greensboro, NC: New Growth Press, 2011.

Tripp, Paul David. *Instruments in the Redeemer's Hands: People in Need of Change Helping People in Need of Change.* Phillipsburg, NJ: P&R, 2002.

Welch, Edward. *When People Are Big and God Is Small: Overcoming Peer Pressure, Codependency, and the Fear of Man.* Phillipsburg, NJ: P&R, 1997.

Wilson, Jared C. *Gospel Wakefulness.* Wheaton, IL: Crossway, 2011.

For more resources on
Gospel-Centered Discipleship go to:
http://www.gospelcentereddiscipleship.com

NOTES

Introduction

1. Joe Thorn, *Note to Self: The Discipline of Preaching to Yourself* (Wheaton, IL: Crossway, 2011).

2. Michael J. Wilkins, *Following the Master: A Biblical Theology of Discipleship* (Grand Rapids, MI: Zondervan, 1992); Jonathan Lunde, *Following Jesus, The Servant King: A Biblical Theology of Covenantal Discipleship* (Grand Rapids, MI: Zondervan, 2010); and portions of Michael Horton, *The Gospel Commission: Recovering God's Strategy for Making Disciples* (Grand Rapids, MI: Baker, 2011).

Chapter 1: Making Disciples

1. The word "disciple" occurs 269 times, whereas "Christian" appears only three times. Luke, the early church historian, uses these terms interchangeably (Acts 11:26). To be a Christian is to be a disciple.

2. Karl Rengstorf comments: "The first time that master and disciple meet on the soil of Greek culture is when Socrates associates with his circle in deliberate avoidance of the teacher-pupil relation which was taken for granted among the Sophists. This is by its very nature rational and professional, and those concerned were in part aware of this. It was now replaced by a purely ideal fellowship between the one who gave out intellectually and those who received intellectually." *Theological Dictionary of the New Testament*, 10 vols., ed. Gerhard Kittel and G. Friedrich, trans. Geoffrey W. Bromiley (Grand Rapids, MI: Eerdmans, 1964–1976), 4:418–21.

3. Michael J. Wilkins, *Following the Master: A Biblical Theology of Discipleship* (Grand Rapids, MI: Zondervan, 1992), 75.

4. Friends and colleagues of the GCM Collective, Jeff Vanderstelt and Caesar Kalinowski, describe a disciple in terms of four "identities": learner, servant, family, and missionary. http://tacoma.somacommunities.org/identity/. My conversations with Jeff have enriched my understanding of what it means to be a disciple.

5. In the article "Missional Discipleship: Reinterpreting the Great Commission," I identify five major commissions. Four of these occur at the end of each Gospel, each emphasizing a different aspect of mission. The fifth commission is the cultural mandate from Genesis 1:26–28. Jonathan K. Dodson, "Missional Discipleship: Reinterpreting the Great Commission," *Boundless,* Feb. 12, 2008, http://www.boundless.org/2005/articles/a0001678.cfm.

6. Contrary to popular interpretation, the "going" participle should not be rendered "as you go," but as "go and disciple the nations." The main point is not to go, or while you are going, but that we are sent to make disciples. See Roy Ciampa, "As you Go, Make Disciples?" Gordon-Conwell Theological Seminary, August 18, 2008, http://connect.gordonconwell.edu/members/blog_view.asp?id=190052&post=37543.

7. Robert E. Coleman, *The Master Plan of Evangelism* (Grand Rapids, MI: Baker, 1963), 21.

8. Throughout church history, the church has attempted to communicate, "all that Christ commanded" through catechesis. The Ten Commandments, the Lord's Prayer, and the Apostles' Creed lay an ethical, spiritual, and doctrinal foundation. Winfield Bev-

ins has appropriated these in a fresh and accessible way for new and renewed disciples in *Creed: Connect to the Basic Essentials of Historic Christian Faith* (Colorado Springs, CO: NavPress, 2011).

9. John Nolland, *The Gospel of Matthew: A Commentary on the Greek Text,* NIGTC (Grand Rapids, MI: Eerdmans, 2005), 1270.

10. In chapter 6 we will talk about these three aspects of a disciple in terms of "conversions." When disciples are centered on the gospel, they experience three conversions, which radically alter their lives.

11. Cited by G. Leibholz in his memoir to Dietrich Bonhoeffer in *The Cost of Discipleship* (New York: Touchstone, 1995), 23.

12. Michael Horton, *The Gospel Commission: Recovering God's Strategy for Making Disciples* (Grand Rapids, MI: Baker, 2011), 176.

13. Scholars refer to this deliberate alignment of Jesus with Yahweh as "Christological monotheism," a phrase coined by N. T. Wright in his article, "Poetry and Theology in Colossians 1:15–20," *NTS* (1990): 444–68.

14. See the frequent mention of Jesus as "Lord" in the greetings of the Pauline epistles and the following key texts: Psalm 110; Hebrews 1; 1 Cor. 8:4–6; Phil. 2:9–11; Col. 1:15–20; 2:6.

15. Richard J. Bauckham helpfully explains Scripture's emphasis on Jesus's divine identity and regal sovereignty by elucidating five things Jesus holds in common with Yahweh: (1) universal sovereign rule and exaltation; (2) exaltation above all angelic powers; (3) bearing the divine name, the tetragrammaton; (4) receives worship; (5) participation in God's unique activity of creation. See *God Crucified: Monotheism and Christology in the New Testament* (Grand Rapids, MI: Eerdmans, 1998), 25–42.

16. For an excellent treatment of the theme of servant, or better "slave of Christ," see Murray J. Harris, *Slave of Christ: A New Testament Metaphor for Total Devotion to Christ* (Downers Grove, IL: InterVarsity, 1999).

17. In the Roman Empire it was ordinary for sentenced men to carry crosses to their executions. Bearing the cross publically displayed a criminal's *submission* to the state, his humbling before the governing authorities. It's like wearing a sign that says: "You thought you could outwit the authorities, but we caught you and now you must humble yourself before us." Taking up a cross, initially, isn't death; it is submission to the governing authorities. For a disciple to take up his cross, then, is not merely an act of *self-denial* but, more importantly, *submission* to Jesus as your governing authority, as your Lord. It is saying no to being your own authority, following yourself, and yes to Jesus's authority—no to your own will and yes to his will.

18. Bonhoeffer, *The Cost of Discipleship*, 89.

19. This helpful saying was coined by Neil Cole, *Organic Church: Growing Faith Where Life Happens* (San Francisco, CA: Jossey-Bass, 2005), 177.

20. Integrated discipleship produces a piety that sends disciples toward sinners, not away from them. It creates what Alan and Debra Hirsch call "missional holiness." Missional holiness was most visible in Jesus. Have you ever noticed that Jesus compelled, not repelled, sinners? He ate with sinners and tax gatherers (Luke 15:1–2). The religious gave him the moniker "friend of sinners" (Luke 7:34). Jesus's holiness was missional. The Hirsches write: "The holiness of Jesus, it seems, is a redemptive, *missional*, world-embracing holiness that does not separate itself from the world, but rather liberates it." When Jesus Christ is our Lord, we will become who we are in Christ (holy) and, consequently, we will live more like him (missionally). Integrated disciples will not choose be-

tween holiness and mission. They choose Christ! See Alan and Debra Hirsch, *Untamed: Reactivating a Missional Form of Discipleship* (Grand Rapids, MI: Baker, 2010), 45–46.

Chapter 2: The Goal of Discipleship

1. Josh Jackson, "Signs of Life and Death," *Paste*, October 2008.

2. C. S. Lewis points out that our desire to be noticed is part of humanity's inconsolable secret, a secret that only God can console: "We should hardly dare to ask that any notice be taken of ourselves. But we pine. The sense that in this universe we are treated as strangers, at the longing to be acknowledged, to meet with some response, to bridge some chasm that yawns between us and reality is part of our inconsolable secret." C. S. Lewis, *The Weight of Glory and Other Addresses* (New York: HarperOne, 2001), 40.

3. For an insightful, biblical examination of this theme see: G. K. Beale, *We Become What We Worship: A Biblical Theology of Idolatry* (Downers Grove, IL: InterVarsity, 2008).

4. J. P. Moreland and Dallas Willard, *Loving God with All Your Mind: The Role of Reason in the Life of the Soul* (Colorado Springs, CO: NavPress, 1997), 12.

5. Thayer's Greek Lexicon in BibleWorks software 6.0.

6. Hymenaeus and Alexander had rejected faith in the gospel and opted for faith in something else. By rejecting Christ, they placed themselves in the hands of Satan. By "handing them over," Paul exercises church discipline that is remedial, not retributive. The hope is that these brothers will repent and return to Christ and his church to continue fighting the good fight of faith. Elsewhere, Paul makes the point that when anyone is outside the church, they are inside Satan's house (2 Cor. 4:4; cf. 1 John 3:8–10). This striking, spiritual contrast reveals how serious God is about sin and grace.

Chapter 3: Twisted Motives

1. I originally worked out some of these ideas regarding accountability in a seminal article entitled, "Accountability Groups," *The JBC* 24 (Spring 2006): 47–52.

2. For an excellent treatment of the God-centered aspect of sin see: Stephen Witmer, "A God-Centered Understanding of Sin," *Reformation 21* (June 2010), http://www.reformation21.org/articles/a-godcentered-understanding-of-sin.php.

3. This gospel truth of Christ as our advocate is the result of his office as a priest on behalf of God's people. For more on the present ministry of Christ as our great high priest, read Hebrews 2–10.

4. This gospel truth is based on the doctrine of justification, which is explained at length in Romans 3–5 and Gal. 2:15–3:29. Justification explains how a just God can accept unjust people and remain just. To put it another way, it is how God can make unrighteous people righteous without compromising his righteousness. I have stated this more simply by saying that Jesus impresses God with his righteousness on our behalf, so that God can accept otherwise unimpressive, unrighteous sinners. For further study, see Mark A. Seifrid, *Christ, Our Righteousness: Paul's Theology of Justification* (Downers Grove, IL: InterVarsity, 2001).

5. Ray LaMontagne, "How Come," *Trouble*, RCA, 2004, compact disc.

6. This gospel truth is based on our status as "slaves of Christ," which is explained in Romans 7, 1 Corinthians 7, and Eph. 6:6. For further study, see Murray J. Harris, *Slave of Christ: A New Testament Metaphor for Total Devotion to Christ* (Downers Grove, IL: InterVarsity, 2001) or, for a more accessible book, John F. MacArthur, *Slave: The Hidden Truth about Your Identity in Christ* (Nashville, TN: Thomas Nelson, 2010).

Notes

Chapter 4: Gospel Motivation

1. Dane Ortlund, *A New Inner Relish: Christian Motivation in the Thought of Jonathan Edwards* (Fearn, Scotland: Christian Focus, 2008) summarizes motivations in three areas—past (gratitude), present (identity), future (personal benefit). Ortlund supports these helpful categories primarily through the writings of Jonathan Edwards. This is a helpful book on the much-neglected topic of motivation.

2. Jonathan Edwards, *A Treatise Concerning Religious Affections, in Three Parts*, vol. 1 *The Works of Jonathan Edwards*, (Carlisle, PA: Banner of Truth, 1995), 277.

3. Ibid., 280.

4. John Piper, *Desiring God: Meditations of a Christian Hedonist* (Colorado Springs, CO: Multnomah, 2003), 12.

5. Piper states: "Delight in the glory of God is not the whole of what faith is." John Piper, *Future Grace* (Colorado Springs, CO: Multnomah, 2005), 203.

6. See John Piper, *When I Don't Desire God: How to Fight for Joy* (Wheaton, IL: Crossway, 2004).

7. For a helpful book that addresses how the warnings of Scripture and our assurance of faith fit together, see Thomas R. Schreiner, *Run to Win the Prize: Perseverance in the New Testament* (Wheaton, IL: Crossway, 2010).

8. As quoted by John Piper when teaching through the TBI seminar "Faith in Future Grace."

9. Tim Chester, *You Can Change: God's Transforming Power for Our Sinful Behavior and Negative Emotions* (Nottingham, UK: Inter-Varsity, 2008), 123.

10. Scripture frequently uses repentance in a way that implies faith (Luke 5:32; Rom 2:4; 2 Cor. 7:10). Other times, repentance and faith are stated explicitly together (Acts 3:19; 20:21).

11. For a gospel-rich explanation of repentance from "gods" see Timothy Keller, *Counterfeit Gods: The Empty Promises of Money, Sex, and Power, and the Only Hope That Matters* (New York: Dutton, 2009).

12. Timothy Keller, "All of Life is Repentance," Redeemer Presbyterian Church, http://download.redeemer.com/pdf/learn/resources/All_of_Life_Is_Repentance-Keller.pdf.

13. Similarly, Keller writes: "In the gospel the purpose of repentance is to *repeatedly tap into the joy of union with Christ* in order to weaken our need to do anything contrary to God's heart" (emphasis added). Ibid., 1.

Chapter 5: Gospel Power

1. For more on this debate, see Wayne Grudem, ed., *Are Miraculous Gifts for Today? Four Views* (Grand Rapids, MI: Zondervan, 1996).

2. All references to Owen's writings are from John Owen, *The Works of John Owen*, ed. William Goold, 24 vols. (Edinburgh and London: Johnstone & Hunter, 1850–1853; repr. vols. 1–16, London: Banner of Truth, 1965).

3. Owen, *The Holy Spirit: His Gifts and Power*, in Ibid., 3:152.

4. Ibid., 371. Furthermore, he writes: "It is too high an impudency for any one to pretend an owning of the gospel, and yet to deny a work of the Holy Ghost in our sanctification," 387.

5. Although Galatians is frequently cited on the subject of justification, it is equally a letter about the person and role of the Spirit. In fact, Paul frames the issue of justification with the Spirit (3:2; 5:25) in order to show that those who are justified by faith in

Christ are necessarily sanctified by reliance on the Spirit. It is through faith in the gospel of Jesus (3:1–9) that we receive the Spirit (3:14) and become sons of the Father (4:1–7).

6. Will Walker, "Learning: The Lost Art of Making People Feel Stupid," in *Postcards from Corinth: Revisiting Discipleship*, ed. Rick James and Betty Churchill (Orlando, FL: CRU), 5–6.

7. Francis Chan, *Forgotten God: Reversing the Tragic Neglect of the Holy Spirit* (Colorado Springs, CO: David C. Cook, 2009).

8. Richard F. Lovelace, *Dynamics of Spiritual Life: An Evangelical Theology of Renewal* (Downers Grove, IL: InterVarsity, 1977).

9. In addition to *Dynamics of Spiritual Life*, see Richard F. Lovelace, *Renewal as a Way of Life: A Guidebook for Spiritual Growth* (Eugene, OR: Wipf & Stock, 2002). The latter is a condensed version of the former and contains more emphasis on spiritual formation.

10. Colin E. Gunton, *The Triune Creator: A Historical and Systematic Study* (Grand Rapids, MI: Eerdmans, 1998).

11. This definition adapted from John Owen, *Communion with the Triune God*, ed. Kelly M. Kapic and Justin Taylor (Wheaton, IL: Crossway, 2007), 93.

12. Owen, *The Holy Spirit*, 523.

Chapter 6: Communal Discipleship

1. For a helpful introduction to gospel community see: Tim Chester and Steve Timmis, *Total Church: A Radical Reshaping around Gospel and Community* (Wheaton, IL: Crossway, 2008).

2. Haydn Schwedland, e-mail to author, February 24, 2011.

3. For a helpful examination of various reasons for church decline from a gospel-centered perspective see Michael Horton, *Christless Christianity: The Alternative Gospel of the American Church* (Grand Rapids, MI: Baker, 2008).

4. I will use church and community interchangeably. This does not mean that I view them as one and the same. All church should be communal, but not all community is church. The whole of church is more than community, including things like mission, biblical leadership, and gospel ministry.

5. Although I have developed the "stature of Christ" biblically and theologically, I owe the initial insight to Andrew F. Walls, who writes: "The very height of Christ's full stature is reached only by the coming together of the different cultural entities into the body of Christ. Only 'together' not on our own, can we reach his full stature." Andrew F. Walls, *The Cross-Cultural Process in Christian History: Studies In the Transmission and Appropriation of Faith* (Maryknoll, NY: Orbis, 2002), 72–81.

6. Tim Chester and Steve Timmis describe this as "three-strand evangelism" in *Total Church*, 60–62.

7. Kristin Vasquez, e-mail to author, March 1, 2011.

8. For a striking treatment of this biblical theme see: G. K. Beale, *The Temple and the Church's Mission: A Biblical Theology of the Dwelling Place of God* (Downers Grove, IL: InterVarsity, 2004). Beale convincingly argues that the garden of Eden in Genesis 2 was meant to be viewed as a kind of garden-temple, and that the patriarchs, Israel, and the church are all called to participate in the global expansion of God's temple through the proclamation of the gospel.

9. Dietrich Bonhoeffer, *Life Together: The Classic Exploration of Faith in Community* (New York: HarperCollins, 1954), 27.

Notes

Chapter 7: Practical Discipleship

1. *Fight Club*, directed by David Fincher (Century City, CA: Fox 2000 Pictures, 1999), VHS.

2. Josh Jackson, "Catching Up with Chuck Palahmuk," *Paste*, September 26, 2008.

3. Richard F. Lovelace, *Dynamics of Spiritual Life: An Evangelical Theology of Renewal* (Downers Grove, IL: InterVarsity, 1979), 89–90.

4. For a set of helpful questions, read through David Powlison's "X-ray Questions," which help get to lies we believe, in *Seeing with New Eyes: Counseling and the Human Condition Through the Lens of Scripture* (Phillipsburg, NJ: P&R, 2003).

5. Timothy Keller elaborates on this concept in *Counterfeit Gods: The Empty Promises of Money, Sex, and Power, and the Only Hope That Matters* (New York: Dutton, 2009).

6. See chapter 4, "Gospel Motives," to see how Jesus fought false promises with true promises.

7. This analogy is original to Oscar Cullmann, *Christ and Time: The Primitive Christian Conception of Time and History*, rev. ed., trans. Floyd V. Filson (Philadelphia, PA: Westminster John Knox Press, 1964), 84, cited in Lee C. Camp, *Mere Discipleship: Radical Christianity in a Rebellious World* (Grand Rapids, MI: Brazos, 2003), 71. For a fuller treatment of this idea, known as inaugurated eschatology, see George Eldon Ladd, *The Presence of the Future: The Eschatology of Biblical Realism* (Grand Rapids, MI: Eerdmans, 1996).

8. Paul exposes this lie with a series of questions: "Are we to continue in sin that grace may abound? By no means! How can we who died to sin still live in it?" (Rom. 6:1–2). Paul's thundering negative is followed by gospel logic. If we have died to sin with Christ, and received his new life, then as new men sin will bother us to the point of repentance. For disciples, sin is a theological absurdity. New men don't live like old men, hobbling around on canes when they can be running marathons.

9. John Owen, *Of the Mortification of Sin in Believers*, vol. 6, *The Works of John Owen*, ed. William Goold, 24 vols. (Edinburgh and London: Johnstone & Hunter, 1850–1853; repr. vols. 1–16, London: Banner of Truth, 1965), 4.

10. Ibid., 9.

11. For a very helpful book on the life of faith, grounded in biblical theology, see Scott J. Hafemann, *The God of Promise and the Life of Faith: Understanding the Heart of the Bible* (Wheaton, IL: Crossway, 2001), 215.

12. John Owen, *The Holy Spirit: His Gifts and Power*, vol. 3, *The Works of John Owen*, 363.

13. Here are a few recommendations from introductory to more advanced: Robert Plummer, *40 Questions about Interpreting the Bible* (Grand Rapids, MI: Kregel, 2010); Gordon D. Fee and Douglas K. Stuart, *How to Read the Bible for All Its Worth: A Guide to Understanding the Bible* (Grand Rapids, MI: Zondervan, 2003); Graeme Goldsworthy, *Gospel-Centered Hermeneutics: Foundations and Principles of Evangelical Biblical Interpretation* (Downers Grove, IL: InterVarsity, 2007); Greg Beale, ed., *The Right Doctrine from the Wrong Text?* (Grand Rapids, MI: Baker, 1994).

Chapter 8: Gospel-Centered Culture

1. Mike Wilkerson, "About," *Redemption* blog, http://www.redemptiongroups.com/what-is-a-redemption-group/.

2. Rick White, e-mail to author, February 24, 2011.

Appendix 1

1. Sam Storms, *A Sincere and Pure Devotion to Christ: 100 Daily Meditations on 2 Corinthians* (Wheaton, IL: Crossway, 2010), 193–94.

DISCUSSION QUESTIONS

Introduction

1. Why is it so important for the gospel to be central in discipleship?
2. What kind of disciples do we make when we share our faith but not our failures?
3. How does your experience of discipleship compare with the author's story?
4. What are you hoping to get out of this book? How will your group commit to applying what you are learning together?

Chapter 1

1. Share what you thought discipleship was prior to reading this chapter. Has your view changed in light of what you read?
2. What are the three aspects of a disciple's identity? Which aspect comes most naturally to you and which one is most challenging?
3. Why is it dangerous to separate evangelism from discipleship?
4. Do you tend to lean towards being a vertical (piety-centered) disciple or a horizontal (mission-centered) disciple? What are some practical ways you can help one another grow towards being a more diagonal (integrated) disciple?

Chapter 2

1. What "cause" are you willing to fight for? Where do you spend your extra time, energy, and effort? What does this misguiding fighting reveal about your heart?
2. How does the reality of who you are compare to the image you project yourself to be? In what way has social media (Facebook, Twitter, blogs) further exposed our tendency to project this false image of ourselves?
3. How does the gospel correct our image?
4. What can this group do to help point one another to beholding and becoming the image of Jesus?

Discussion Questions

Chapter 3

1. Do you tend to gravitate towards being the religious person who verbally punishes others for failing to keep the rules or the rebellious person who is quick to overlook one another's failure? How do both of these prove inadequate?

2. Consider Psalm 32:3–4. Does anyone in the group have trouble confessing sin with honesty? What are we robbing ourselves of when we fail to confess our sins to each other and God?

3. How is confession of sin repentance from being inauthentic?

4. Do you find yourself falling into religious performance or spiritual license? How can you help one another avoid these extremes and center on Christ?

Chapter 4

1. Why is it essential for us to move beyond addressing outward actions and get to heart motivations? How can this group help one another do this?

2. Discuss how you have previously viewed religious affections? In what ways did the chapter challenge your previous view and in what way did it affirm it?

3. Have you taken a sober look at the warnings in Scripture? What are the sins in your life that you take lightly and need to be warned away from? Take some time and ask the Spirit to show each person in the group areas that they are failing to heed God's warnings concerning sin.

4. How can your group promote earnest, life-giving repentance with one another? What does it look like for you to help each other turn from sin to Christ?

Chapter 5

1. In what ways have you neglected the person of the Holy Spirit in your life? What would it look like for this group to be led by the Spirit together?

2. How did Jesus live in relation to the Holy Spirit during his time on earth? What can we learn and apply from this?

3. How would walking in dependence on the Spirit change the way we view the events that come up each day?

4. Do you interact with the Spirit as a person? How are you learning to recognize the Spirit's voice and respond with obedience?

Chapter 6

1. How can you relate to Hadyn's story of being converted to Christ but not community or mission? Take some time to share your own story with respect to the "three conversions" mentioned in this chapter.

2. Do you consider others before yourself in your community? What would this look like practically? Discuss some real life examples of people who reflect the selflessness of Christ.

3. How is God calling you to reorient your life to be in steady community that is gathered around the gospel and sent out on mission? List specific barriers that keep you from this and have your group talk you through each of them.

Chapter 7

1. Pick a sin you struggle with and consider the what, when, and why surrounding it in order to know your sin.

2. Where should our power to fight sin come from? When we fight sin, what are we truly fighting for?

3. Write down the lie you tend to believe and a counter, gospel promise you can believe. Share your gospel homework with one another and discuss.

4. Pick a passage of Scripture and do Text-Theology-Life. Share with your group.

Chapter 8

1. What are some ways you can keep the gospel central in discipleship?

2. How can you share your stories of gospel change with others?

3. Set a regular time to begin your fight club to fight for the noble, glorious image of Christ to be revealed in one another!

GENERAL INDEX

SCRIPTURE INDEX